# BARRYMORE

# BARRYMORE

## A Man Possessed

PHIL TAYLOR &
PAUL NICHOLAS

metro

Published by Metro Publishing Ltd, 3 Bramber Court,
2 Bramber Road, London W14 9PB, England

First published in hardback in 2002

ISBN 1 843580 31 4

British Library Cataloguing-in-Publication Data: A catalogue record
for this book is available from the British Library.

Design by ENVY

Printed and bound in Great Britain by CPD (Wales)

1 3 5 7 9 10 8 6 4 2

Papers used by Metro Publishing Ltd are natural, recyclable products
made from wood grown in sustainable forests. The manufacturing processes
conform to the environmental regulations of the country of origin

The publishers are grateful to the *News of the World*
for supplying all the photographs used in this book.

# Contents

# THE BODY
# IN THE POOL

IT WAS a cold, clear Friday evening in Bagshot Park, the imperiously grand country seat of Prince Edward and his bride Sophie Wessex. Sophie stood at the window, looked out over her estate in the growing gloom, glanced at her watch and ticked off the hours. The day before, wearing the black-and-white pearl earrings her husband had commissioned especially for their wedding day, Sophie had sat in the Regency Drawing Room at Buckingham Palace and given the most revealing interview of her life to a *News of the World* journalist. She had sipped tea from a bone china cup and, against the whirring of the Queen's helicopter landing in the garden and the yapping of the corgis going to meet her, had said more than anyone had expected her to.

'My Edward is not gay,' she'd insisted, giving voice to a persistent rumour about her husband's sexuality.

Now, on Friday night, there were fewer than thirty-six hours until her interview would hit the streets. Other papers would pick it up, she was certain. And now Sophie imagined her face filling the front page and wondered what the reaction from the Queen would be. Not to mention her husband.

About seventy miles away, in Essex, Michael Barrymore looked out of his window at the darkening sky and checked his watch. He sipped a Jack Daniel's and Sprite, his favourite combination. He'd even named his dogs after the drink. They weren't corgis, like the Queen's, but they still made enough of a noise when they got boisterous. He too had heard the rumours about Edward being gay. Who hadn't? But he was certain they weren't true. Anyway, Michael had problems about his own sexuality to contend with. One boyfriend had just walked out of his life and another one, John Kenney, had taken his place. John worked at an estate agency in north London. Michael had rung him a few hours earlier, just for a chat. He got so lonely on his own that he'd call time and time again, just to hear a friendly voice. John suggested going out for a meal that night. That cheered up Michael no end; he hated staying in. And even when they'd finished eating, the night would still be young by Michael's standards. Maybe they could go on somewhere…

Michael took a sip of his drink. It felt like an old friend as it swirled in his mouth. He poured himself another slug of bourbon, then ambled over to the massive fridge in his kitchen and topped up his glass with Sprite, splashing a little on the black granite work surface.

Within the next ten hours or so, fate would move in a way no one could have expected. The pieces were already in place and the life stories of Sophie, Countess of Wessex and Michael Barrymore, one of Britain's favourite entertainers, were both about to become front-page news.

That Saturday – March 31, 2001 – the newsrooms of every Sunday newspaper were as busy as usual, though those of the *News of the World* were busier than most. They had the exclusive Sophie interview. Pages 1, 2, 3, 4 and 5 had already been earmarked. Then, at 12.21 precisely on Saturday afternoon, a news item marked 'Urgent' popped on to computer screens from the Press Association. It was what used to be called a newsflash: 'A man died in hospital today after he was found unconscious in a swimming pool at the home of entertainer Michael Barrymore, Essex Police said.'

The man's name was Stuart Lubbock. Further reports would suggest that Stuart was dead when he was pulled out of the pool. As details emerged, it became clear that this wasn't going to be one of those stories about outrages that took place in a mansion when the star owner was away. Michael had been very much there. He was the host, he'd seen Stuart's half-naked body floating in the pool.

Within thirty minutes, Page 1 was recast. Sophie Wessex found herself sharing the front page with a gay man whose tragedy she could never have imagined. Since the early hours of that Saturday morning Michael Barrymore's life had changed forever... and Stuart Lubbock's devastated mother was mourning the terrible loss of a son, his girlfriend the death of a partner and the father of her children.

Three people were better placed than anyone to describe what went on that night at the Barrymore mansion. They were: John Kenney; a dustman called Justin Merritt who had been invited back to Michael's mansion and was among the first to arrive... and Michael himself. Three very different testimonies to one awful tragedy.

For John Kenney, the night of Friday March 30 began with that phone call to the West Hampstead estate agency. (He had worked there ever since moving to London from Blackpool to be with Michael.) John recalled: 'I spoke to Michael four or five times that day, which was normal. He rang me at 4 p.m. and asked what time I was finishing, because his neighbour Gary Jones, Gary's wife Denise and their three kids wanted to come over. Michael always has people over and loves playing the host because he hates being on his own. Then Michael added with a chuckle, "I've got a surprise for you when you get home." When I asked what it was, he said I'd have to wait until I arrived.'

The next phone call John took at his desk was also to contain a surprise – though that would be putting it mildly. 'Shock' might be a better description. Mike 'Brownie' Brown, Michael's personal assistant, wanted John to sign a contract covering his time with Michael.

John explained: 'Brownie phoned me and said, "Now you and Michael are really serious, I need you to sign a confidentiality agreement." He's a bit of a wind-up merchant, so I laughed and told him to shut up. But when I realised he was serious, I was very offended. Brownie told me that everyone in Michael's company, or anyone surrounding him, has to sign one. And I said, "Well, I've got a prenuptial agreement – he can sign that."

'I even got a solicitor friend to help me word it. It included the clauses like, whoever is in the bath last has to wash it; don't leave dirty laundry on the floor; if anything happens to the relationship you walk out with what you walked into it with; and to have at least one early night a week. I even printed it out to take home with me and show Michael.'

John left the office at 6.15 p.m. and, fifteen minutes later, dropped by Gary's work in Kentish Town to give him a lift home. By 7.45 p.m. they were back in Roydon, Essex, where Michael had the palatial spread that would soon become notorious as the mansion of death. As John walked through the door, Michael was already showered and dressed in a casual top and jeans. The Jack Daniel's was gone and by now he had a glass of Chablis Premier Cru in his hand.

'I asked Gary if he, Denise and their children wanted to join us for dinner,' John explained. 'He suggested an Indian restaurant in Broxbourne, which is about a fifteen-minute drive away, over the county border in Hertfordshire. I asked him to order a cab while I got ready. Then I walked into the kitchen and told Michael that Brownie had called me about the confidentiality agreement.

'I got the "pre-nup" out of my folder and handed it to Michael and said to him, "Well, if I've got to sign one of those, this is for you." He read it and burst out laughing. Then he read it to Brownie over the phone.'

The humour made the issue of the confidentiality agreement seem rather redundant. 'That was the last time anything like that was mentioned,' said John. At the time, of course, he couldn't have realised how important his failure to sign the document would become. It left him free to reveal publicly what went on in the mansion that night.

By 9 p.m., Michael, John, Gary and Gary's family had taken a cab to the Bengali Indian restaurant in Broxbourne. 'The whole plan was to have a nice quiet meal out with our friends,' said John. 'We ordered a lot of food – a main course each and loads of extras that came on a trolley with rice and naan bread. We were drinking Chablis, Michael's favourite, and he just seemed to pick at the dishes after he'd finished his main course.

'I remember that during the meal, a couple of Essex girls with blonde hair and long red fingernails came in and started talking to us. But by midnight we'd decided to leave. The taxi that came to pick us up was a people carrier, and on the way home Michael suggested going to a nightclub. He asked Gary to come with us but Denise said no.'

It would turn out to be the best decision that Denise and Gary Jones had ever made.

Now that Michael had decided he was going to party, nothing could dissuade him – the only remaining question was where. 'Michael was talking to the driver, who suggested a club in Harlow,' said John. 'It was called the Millennium.' Within the next twenty-four hours this club would become one of the most talked about and photographed venues in the land.

'I was pretty drunk by this stage and I must admit I was up for a club,' John continued. 'We dropped Gary and his family off home and between 12.30 a.m. and 1 a.m. Michael and I got to the Millennium nightclub, though I hadn't been paying much attention to the route we were taking and I couldn't have honestly said at the time which town we were in. But anyway, the doormen recognised Michael and ushered us in immediately. We went straight to the bar.' Essex was the heartland of Michael's fan base, the people who watched *Strike It Lucky* and dreamed of being on the show themselves. Michael was their hero, a star in their midst. And that night in the club, they were going to make the most of it.

'Suddenly, people came from everywhere, swarming around Michael,' John went on. 'They were shouting his name and all trying to talk to him. It was very dark in there with very loud music and flashing lights. Really, it was irritating me and I sobered up pretty quickly in there. As I recall, three bouncers came over to stand near Michael to protect him in case there was any trouble. We only had a couple of drinks together, our usual Jack Daniel's and Sprite, because we couldn't move with so many people around us.'

But one man in particular was spotted joking with his idol. By now Michael had moved on from the JD and Sprite and was swigging bottles of powerful Vodka Kick. His companion turned out to be a butchery worker named Stuart Lubbock.

Engineer Mike Crook was one of Stuart's pals. Mike, twenty-one, recalled: 'He and Michael had sat chatting for ages in the club and they were obviously getting on. Michael told me he was going back to his house for a few more drinks and asked if I wanted to come. I said no because I had to work the next day. But Stuart came up to me and said, "I can't believe I've pulled Michael Barrymore." Stuart's never had a problem with being bisexual – he told me about it quite openly the first time we met. He was always up for a laugh.'

Another pal, a window cleaner named Carl Williams, said Stuart was drunk and high on drugs that night. 'Stuart was really buzzing ,' said 31-year-old Carl. 'And judging by his behaviour and what he'd normally do on a Saturday, I think he must have popped a couple of pills, probably Ecstasy. He'd drunk Stella as well. He must have had a lot, because his eyes were all over the place.'

Carl had been sitting with Stuart when he and Michael had exchanged their first pleasantries in the Millennium Club. 'Stuart was really happy Barrymore had come over to our table,' he went on. 'He must have spoken to Stuart for about fifteen minutes. I don't know what they were talking about, but there was a lot of laughing and they were obviously getting on well. Stuart later introduced me and I remember Michael shook my hand and put his other hand around the back of my head, rubbing it in a friendly sort of way.'

But when Stuart later told Carl that he too had been invited to the Michael's house for a party, Carl refused to go with him. In his case, however, it was a decision he would come to regret for the rest of his days. He was seeing his friend Stuart for the last time.

'Stuart was really excited,' Carl went on. 'I was a little bit more scared. If I'd been drunk I'd have just said yes. But I was worried about what might be on the agenda, so I wanted to be able to leave and get a cab when I wanted to. But I only had £7 and I reckoned I needed £10 for the fare home. So I refused to go. Stuart should still be alive, and if I'd gone back to Barrymore's he might have been. I wasn't drunk or high on drugs. I was thinking straight. I'd have looked after Stuart, as you do when a mate is really off his head.

'It all came down to that extra £3 for the taxi. That's what made the difference. It wouldn't have happened if I was there. I wouldn't have let it.'

John Kenney estimates that he and Michael eventually left the club sometime between 2 a.m. and 3 a.m. But as they got outside and felt the cold March air hit them, John realised that they'd left their jackets in the club cloakroom. 'I said to Michael, "Hang on, I'll go back and get them,"' he recalled. 'But when I got back outside, I couldn't find Michael anywhere. I panicked. I didn't really know where I was and I was frantically looking for Michael. He'd simply vanished.

'Then two girls came out of the club and one of them said, "Oh you're Michael's boyfriend, aren't you? He's gone off with a couple of lads." I asked where but they didn't know, they assumed Michael had probably gone off to one of the boys' flats in Harlow.'

John hadn't thought there was a need to check with the taxi driver where they were being taken – he was just going with the flow. He assumed he'd simply be taken back to Roydon again, which was somewhere not too far away – though his geography of Essex was a bit hazy. Now he was totally disorientated.

He recalled: 'I asked the girls, "Where am I?" When they said Harlow, I said, "Where's Harlow?" Then one of the girls said, "One of the lads was Justin Merritt, we know his sister. I'll ring her and find out where they are." She got through to Justin's sister, who I discovered was called Kylie. By luck Kylie had also gone off with Michael in his party group. She explained that they were already all back at Michael's house which, it turned out, was only ten minutes away.'

By now the two girls John was talking to were becoming fascinated by the unfolding events of the night. You didn't usually get a lot of celebrity interest in the Millennium car park, and they weren't going to let go of John in a hurry.

He continued: 'I got a cab back to Roydon with the two girls. To be honest, I invited them back just in case Michael wasn't at home and we had to look elsewhere. I was absolutely furious that Michael has just abandoned me. Worse, I didn't have my mobile because I'd left it at Michael's.'

Cab driver Keith Herrett, who had driven Michael home, later revealed: 'Barrymore was clearly the worse for wear and was unsteady on his feet. They all seemed up for a party.'

When John arrived, he was still fuming and marched straight into the kitchen. There he found Michael holding court with Justin Merritt, sister Kylie and a man he later discovered was Stuart Lubbock, although John and he were never introduced.

Police estimate that Stuart, who lived in Great Bray, near Harlow, had arrived at the mansion at about 2.30 a.m.

'There is a semi-circular granite worktop in the middle of the kitchen which has a stainless steel hob on it,' said John. 'There are five stools around it and usually guests sit there while Michael wanders around playing host. When I came into the kitchen, he looked up and casually said hello. I don't remember the time exactly but by now it must have been between 3 a.m. and 4 a.m.'

John wasn't ready for pleasantries. 'I turned around and walked into the bedroom,' he said. 'Michael followed me in and we started to argue. I said to him, "Who are these people? You've invited these people back to the house and you don't even know who they are."

'Michael insisted, "I do" then added sarcastically, "Oh shut up. You sound like Shaun", meaning Shaun Davis his ex-boyfriend. I said, "Fine", but I was seething. There was no point talking to him because he was drunk. Michael and I went back into the kitchen and just then the video intercom buzzed.

'I could see two lads standing at the electronic front gate. "Who's that?" I asked Michael. "Oh, they're two lads from the village," he answered. I'd never seen them at the house before but he let them in anyway. I was still very angry but thought I might as well get to know these people if they were staying.

'Justin, the man who had already been in the kitchen when I came in, introduced himself. He kept telling me what a nice guy

I was and we were getting on well. That's when I asked him if he fancied a dip in the Jacuzzi and offered him some shorts. We went to the main bedroom to get changed.'

John and Justin then stepped outside. It was icy cold, but the warm water in the Jacuzzi was steaming. They quickly slid in until the water covered their shoulders.

'You can step from the Jacuzzi on to a ledge and into the pool,' explained John. 'Justin and I were just sitting chatting while the water bubbled around us. Then Kylie came out and brought me a glass of white wine and a can of lager for her brother. She sat on the edge of the Jacuzzi's blue mosaic tiles to my right, just chatting. We were talking about where we were from, what we did for a living. I asked Justin, who was sitting to my left, "How long have you known Michael?" And he said, "Oh I've only met him tonight."

'From where I sat in the Jacuzzi, I could see through the doorway into the kitchen where Michael was wandering around. I spotted Stuart Lubbock, the two girls I'd brought back with me, and the two lads from the village who'd appeared at the gate. They all just seemed to be chatting and drinking. I could hear music coming from the lounge.'

Minutes later, said John, Stuart emerged from the house in a pair of shorts. They would later be identified as grey boxer shorts, marked 'Outfit' on the label. 'At that time all I could see was that they were dark coloured,' said John. 'He walked over to the Jacuzzi and got in with us. He was mumbling about something, but I couldn't understand what he was saying and I looked at Justin, puzzled. Stuart was sitting opposite me and he suddenly slumped forward, his face drooping into the water. I said, "Oi! Sober yourself up", and pushed him up to stop him falling into the water. He was swaying all over the place but eventually he sat back. I simply thought he was drunk. It didn't enter my head that he might have been on drugs.'

By now it was getting too cold even to stay in the warm Jacuzzi. Shivering, John suggested to Justin that it was time to go inside and dry off. 'We got out and left Stuart in there,' he said. 'He just sat back and stretched his elbows to the side, like he was making himself comfortable. That was my last image of him alive. Now I think back, we probably should have got him out.'

Back in Michael's bedroom, John and Justin towelled off and got dressed. It was then, said John, that he heard a commotion in the hallway.

'The two blonde girls who came back with me were running up the hallway laughing and carrying on,' he said. 'They came into the bedroom and started going through the drawers and touching Michael's clothes in the wardrobe. I said to them, "Do you mind? That's very rude." Then they went out again.

'I'd put some music on the stereo in the bedroom, which is on the opposite side of the house to the lounge. I suppose Justin and I were in there for about fifteen minutes, just chatting.'

But the chatting ended when Michael burst into the room, yelling. Paling at the memory, John recalled: 'He shouted, "John! Someone's floating in the pool!" He knew I had training in CPR [cardio pulmonary resuscitation]. Justin, Kylie and I raced outside to see what was going on.'

'I went outside through the door, which leads to the left side of the pool, and Stuart was lying on the paving on the right side of the pool near the sun loungers. I don't know who got him out of the water but he was lying there flat on his back. I know Michael wouldn't have got him out because he's scared of water and only ever goes in waist deep.

'I can still see it. Stuart had his eyes wide open and the back of his head facing towards the house. All I saw was his face. I just went into autopilot, though I'd never seen a dead body like that before. Sure, I'd worked as an auxiliary nurse and I'd seen geriatrics dead, but peacefully dead. Stuart's eyes were fixed and wide open.'

Jolting himself into action, John marshalled his thoughts. 'You have to think ABC,' he said. 'Airways, breathing and circulation. I turned Stuart on to his side, but there was nothing there. No breathing, no pulse, nothing. So I put him on his back and as I knelt to his left side, I tipped his head back, pinched the bridge of his nose to force the air into his lungs and gave him two breaths. I crossed my palms over his ribcage and pushed down to give him fifteen compressions.'

After the first two breaths, a frantic John noticed Stuart was bringing up something dark and sticky but he couldn't tell whether it was alcohol or vomit. 'I just carried on,' he said, 'and I remember shouting for someone to dial 999.'

By now, all the guests were outside watching Stuart's life ebb away. All except Michael.

Justin was on the phone to the emergency services and they were giving him instructions,' John went on. 'I could hear him say, "He's already doing that", and they told him I was doing fine.'

Lost in his desperate efforts to revive Stuart, John was yet to notice that Michael had panicked and run away. 'Kylie was next to me,' John continued. 'I told her to get some blankets because Stuart was freezing cold. His whole body was a bluey-grey colour. I later saw a picture of him in the newspaper and I haven't got a clue who that was. That was nothing like the person I saw. I don't know whether he was dead at that point. The thing with CPR is that you just carry on until the ambulance men get there.

'I was totally focused on this poor lad, trying to save his life. Somebody got some towels and wrapped them around Stuart. I was getting very tired but I knew I couldn't give up because there's always a small chance you can find a pulse or get them breathing again.'

In a blaze of sirens and lights, the paramedics burst through the house and told John to continue while they got their equipment set up. 'Then they took over and started shocking him so the electrical charge would start him breathing,' he continued. They were asking for lights because they couldn't see what they were doing. I didn't know where the outside light switch was, so I held a torch over Stuart until they told me to stop. Then the paramedics strapped Stuart to a stretcher and carried him through the house into the ambulance.

'I broke down in tears. For twenty-five minutes I'd tried everything I could but it still wasn't enough to save his life. I didn't even know his name until I read it in the paper the next day. By now the police were already searching the garden for clues.'

It was only now that John finally had the chance to look for Michael. He was nowhere to be seen. John looked in the house and around the grounds. Nothing.

He recalled: 'One of the girls said, "He's gone. He's run out. He left with those two guys to go down to the village. He must have run down the street." I couldn't believe Michael would just run out like that. Then the police asked me whose house it was and where Michael was. I had to admit that I didn't know.'

John confesses himself shocked and disappointed at Michael's actions. 'He showed he has no stamina at all. He's a coward. When the crunch came in a life-or-death situation, the only thing that mattered to Michael was helping himself. That's the way he was and when he couldn't run from something, he hid behind a haze of cocaine, Valium or alcohol.'

Stuart Lubbock was declared dead at 8.32 a.m. by doctors at

Harlow's Princess Alexandra Hospital. Shortly afterwards, Michael's assistant Mike Brown rang John and told him to pack a bag. He was coming to get John out of the house.

'I just wanted to get out of there,' admitted John. 'I wanted to be with Michael. I wanted to know what was going on. Brownie told me he was at some lad's flat in the village. When Brownie arrived he told police where Michael was and they went down to interview him.'

Brownie then drove John to Michael's bolthole. Exhausted, angry and tearful, John lashed out at his lover, demanding answers. 'I went straight up to him and said: "What the f*** happened to you?" said John. 'He looked terrible and he just said, "I freaked. I'm sorry. I ran." Michael tried to put his arm around me and I snapped at him, "Don't even touch me. You're bang out of order." I paused and told him, "You know that lad's dead, don't you?" "Yes," he said quietly.

'Then I asked him, "Well, who was he? Did you know him?" He said no. I couldn't believe what I was hearing. Some lad had died in Michael's pool and neither of us knew him. Michael and I then went to Brownie's house in Brentwood. Michael walked into the lounge and I went into the living room. I couldn't stand to be anywhere near him.

'Brownie's wife Maria was making tea and toast but I was too shocked to have anything. Michael kept looking at me, pleading forgiveness.'

By this stage, news of the death was all over the TV and radio. A spokesman for Michael released a short statement that read: 'Mr Barrymore is very, very upset over this tragic accident and his feelings go out to the young man's family.'

John added: 'Michael gave me a Valium and took one too. My mobile phone was going crazy. My mum had seen it on the news and because it was a lad in his thirties she thought it could be me. She was crying and so relieved when I answered the phone. But eventually the Valium knocked me out and I fell asleep on the sofa with Michael.

'The next thing I knew, Brownie's wife Maria was waking me and saying, "You're going to the Priory with Michael. It's the best place for you." It was about 3.30 on the Saturday afternoon. I looked at Michael and he said, "If we go there they can't get to us", meaning the press. At the time I thought it was for the best, but now I realise that was typical Michael. Something goes wrong and he runs to the Priory.'

Brownie drove the Mercedes, Maria sat in the front with him. 'Michael sat in the back looking at me and occasionally staring at the window,' said John dolefully. 'He could see me crying and kept asking if I was all right. I just wanted to be left alone. What he did was unforgivable. Everyone has their own way of dealing with stress and shock. Obviously he's used to running and hiding.'

# 2

# 'I'M HIV POSITIVE, MICHAEL'

THE FEES for the Marchwood Priory in Southampton would be around £2,500 a week. To Michael, that was a small price to pay. He had people to handle details like that.

By 6 p.m. the two men were in the capable hands of Austin Tate, who runs the place. Michael knew what to expect – by now he was an old hand at visiting clinics like this. John had read of the Priory and the superstar clients it helped. Now he looked around him, at the plain chairs and tables, and wondered who'd sat there before him and waited with bated breath for the treatment to start.

All John knew was that, after the sort of night he'd had, oblivion would come like a welcome friend.

'As soon as Michael and I arrived on the Saturday, we were

given sleeping tablets for later that night,' he said, recalling every detail of those first moments of relative calm as the nation's press hunted high and low for the hottest interview of the moment.

But the calm was only surface-deep. John could not rid himself of the image of Stuart Lubbock floating in the ice-cold pool, or the image of his face just millimetres from his own as he gave him the kiss of life.

'During the next day, the Sunday, I was napping when some nurses rushed in to wake me up because I was screaming and thrashing about in my sleep,' he shuddered. 'I'd have this dream where all I could see was Stuart's blue, dead face.

'For two weeks I felt pretty much incapable of doing anything. I felt that I was cut off from reality. Towards the end, the dosage was reduced to 2 milligrams of Valium four times a day. Michael spent all day in AA meetings because he was being treated for alcoholism and stress, so I just sat in my room or wandered around the grounds.'

The Michael Barrymore that John had met and fallen for was gone, replaced by someone he hardly knew and who had the weight of the world on his shoulders. 'He was a shell of a man,' said John, a cloud of concern etching his features. 'The party host, the man who loved to laugh, the practical joker… all that had well and truly vanished. I'd never seen him like this; to be honest, I never in my darkest moments expected to see him like this. He was very quiet all the time, and that was strange because he'd always been such a chatterbox.

'I was in my own world and he was in his. I felt I needed to look after him and I just wanted Michael to get back to normal. Sure, "normal" for Michael might not have been normal for everyone else, but nevertheless I wanted him to return to the sort of person he used to be.'

John had changed too. In ways that he couldn't tell when he looked in the mirror. But it was clear to his elder sister Denise when she came to visit him. She took one look at her brother – the man once so ebullient that he was happy to perform in gay revues – and could hardly believe her eyes. 'She said that I looked and acted like a zombie,' said John, shaking his head. 'She was probably right.'

But despite the medication that kept the worst of the demons at bay, during daylight hours at least, the long nights of that early spring were the most harrowing time for John. Staff were so concerned that they moved two beds into Michael's room so the two men could be together.

'I generally had the same violent nightmare every night,' John added. 'That image of Stuart's face floating in front of me.'

Through his nightmare all the details would come flooding back, the screams, the shouts down the mobile phone, the flashing lights of the police cars and ambulance... but most of all, the icy tentacles of cold that gripped his fingers as he held Stuart's body at the poolside.

'Often I'd wake Michael and he'd reach over to cuddle me,' John went on. 'He'd put his arms around me and say, "It'll be all right, you'll see."' But in the darkness of the room, John could see the furrows deepening on Michael's face. He knew that things were a long way from being all right.

During that first week at the Priory, TV star Caroline Aherne left a message at reception asking Michael to call her. The actress, who was a national favourite as Mrs Merton and for her part in *The Royle Family*, had some idea what Michael was going through. She too had battled drink and drug problems in the Priory and was ringing to offer him her shoulder to cry on.

'Michael told me he called her back when I was out of the room,' John continued. 'I think he was just glad to have the support.'

Then there was a phone call from John's boss at the estate agency where he worked. It brought back a searing memory of a moment when everything had been normal. John had left his desk without a care in the world on that fateful Friday, thinking only of going out and having some fun that night.

His boss's voice on the phone broke through the reverie. 'How long do you think you'll be at the Priory, John... ' there was a pregnant pause. John knew what was coming. To be honest, he understood perfectly.

'My boss was very nice about it but I said that he should

probably let me go because I didn't know how I was going to cope,' John admitted with a wry smile at his change of fortune. 'I put the phone down with an air of finality. Brownie had come to visit us and he and Michael were in the room at the time. I told them what had happened and that I was effectively out of a job. Brownie came to the rescue. "Don't worry," he told me, "we need a researcher on LWT."'

It was a well-trodden path for a Barrymore boyfriend. Months before, Michael had found TV backroom work for Shaun Davis. At the time Michael had insisted it was a proper job that needed doing, but as he sat in the Priory, in a room paid for by Michael, John was determined to hang on to a shred of independence. 'That offer didn't appeal to me,' he said. 'I really would be doing what Shaun did – going totally into his world and losing my identity.'

After exactly two weeks of treatment, John left the clinic. It was April 14 – a date that Michael too would remember for the rest of his life because of the parting bombshell that John delivered.

He revealed that he was HIV positive.

Every word spoken that day is now imprinted on his memory. 'I was leaving the Priory before Michael,' said John. 'Brownie came into our room as I was packing my things. There was a bit of small talk then he said to me, "Look John, there's no easy way of saying this, but are you HIV positive?"

Michael was in the room too. Everything went deathly quiet. I looked across at Michael and his face was totally shocked. We were both on Valium but you could tell that all his senses were straining for my reply.

'Finally I broke the silence. "Yes," I said simply. Then, turning to Brownie, I asked, "How did you know?" He said that rumours had been doing the rounds. With that he went downstairs to put my bags in the car, leaving Michael and me alone to talk.'

The emotions that Michael must have been feeling can only be guessed at… the memories of every time he and John had slept together, the shared moments on holiday, the nights in his mansion, would have been flicking through his mind. Many times he'd contemplated his death possibly through drink and drugs, but never, ever this way.

John went on: 'Michael was staring at me, transfixed. He asked quietly, "Why didn't you tell me?"'

John stood his ground. He said: 'I looked at Michael and answered, "It's not that I didn't want to tell you. But you know, at the end of the day Michael, you were the one who was quite willing to go ahead without condoms, but I wouldn't."'

John couldn't predict what Michael's response would be – there might have been anger, blind frustration, shouting… Instead, Michael's features softened. He said to John: 'Come on, give me a cuddle.'

But John had steeled himself so much during the course of the conversation that he could not. 'I refused because I didn't know what Michael's next response would be,' he said. 'I didn't want his pity. Michael said, "Please don't push me away", but I really couldn't stay. I had to get away.'

John went downstairs to the car and left Michael trembling at the doorway of their room. He looked so lost and alone that John turned back. 'I went back and gave him that cuddle,' he said. 'I remember that Michael had tears in his eyes. Sadness for me and sadness for himself, I suppose.'

Two days later, accompanied by Michael's lawyer David Corker, John gave a statement to Brentwood CID. He said after giving the statement: 'A detective took a swab of saliva from inside my mouth for a DNA test. They said they weren't satisfied that I'd told them the full picture. The truth is, I've told the police all I know, but I can't say what happened during the party at Michael's house before I arrived.'

John and Michael did not speak for a few days, each wondering how the other felt. But eventually, consumed with worry and with so many questions to ask, Michael could contain himself no longer. He knew that John had returned to Hammersmith to stay with friends, somewhere he could feel comfortable. Michael found a number for John, called him and let all his anxiety pour out.

'How did you catch it?' he asked John, almost not waiting

for an answer. 'Have I got it too? Oh God, no – I'll have to take a test.'

Eventually John had a chance to speak and said that he had contracted the virus during a single night of unprotected sex with a businessman in February 1999. Just nineteen months later, he was diagnosed as HIV positive.

'After my liaison with that man I knew I'd done something stupid,' he confessed. 'Over the next few months I now know I went through something called "serial conversion", which means the virus was attacking the healthy cells in my body. I was covered in a rash and I suffered from night sweats and diarrhoea. I thought I had mouth ulcers, but they were actually oral herpes. Friends of mine had been through it so I knew I'd now caught it myself. I was very angry with myself but I have to live with it.'

Every three months, unknown to Michael, John would go to hospital for blood tests to check his liver function and immune system. 'I didn't tell Michael, because I always insisted we use condoms during intercourse,' he said. 'So I never put him at risk.'

In fact, said John, he seemed to be recklessly putting himself in danger. 'From the very beginning I brought condoms over to the house and put them in the side drawer next to the bed,' he added. 'The first night we had sex I leant over to get them out of the drawer and Michael asked what I was doing. I was amazed. I said, "What does it look like I'm doing? I'm putting a condom on." He seemed surprised when I said I'd brought them.

'On another occasion, when he wanted intercourse, I'd asked him where his condoms were kept and he replied, "I don't use them." I was stunned. Here was a supposedly mature, intelligent man and he was playing Russian roulette with his life.

'Now, during the phone call, when Michael told me he wanted a test, I tried to reassure him and told him he wasn't at risk because we were never unprotected.' But Michael was still worried, and a week later, said John, he did take a medical test while police continued their investigation into the death of Stuart Lubbock.

'Michael phoned me as soon as he got the result, which was about twenty-four hours after he had taken the blood test,' John added. 'He said, "It's OK. The test was negative."' Then he told me, "I spoke to the doctor who gave me the blood test and he said it wasn't such a big deal these days because you can get treatment."' Michael later released a statement through his lawyers to confirm that he had taken an Aids test and that the results had been negative.

On May 11, Michael went home to his mansion for the first time since the night Stuart Lubbock drowned in his pool. He looked pale and thin after six weeks in the Priory. John went to visit him, though their relationship was now clearly strained.

Michael told John plaintively that the police had taken a DNA swab from him too. "'I'm getting pressure from the TV companies," Michael said. "Until they get the results of the DNA tests I can't start back at work. It's all a bit of a mess. But what's the DNA going to show? Nothing.'"

John was annoyed that Michael seemed to be so self-pitying, that this great TV favourite did not realise the pain he was suffering too. 'That night will haunt me for the rest of my life,' John told Michael, pleading for understanding. 'Well it's not going to go away from me either, is it?' replied Michael briskly. 'Yes,' said John, 'but I was the one left at the poolside with a body, wasn't I?' Michael answered: 'I know that, but you're not the one who's going to be responsible for it. It's me.'

Then Michael told John: 'I've been on my own most of the time. I haven't had anybody here. I sent the dogs away because I couldn't handle them being here. I've got people who care for me but there's no more they can do for me if I don't feel in that mood.' He seemed like a very lonely figure at that moment.

After John's HIV confession, he and Michael never again made love, though Michael insisted he still wanted to continue their relationship. The two stopped seeing each other. With the police inquiry into the pool death continuing, Michael told John in a phone call from his mansion: 'I miss you. I thought you were coming back. Are you?' But John, traumatised by all that had taken place, could not return to the kind of life

BARRYMORE

Michael lived and eventually made it clear he never wanted to see Michael again.

'To be honest, I wasn't ever planning to tell anyone about the HIV – mainly to protect Michael,' he said. 'But with all that's come out, I really need to set the record straight about our relationship. I think he was grateful that I insisted on the condoms, but there were times after we finished when I wasn't sure if he'd learned his lesson. Sometimes I'd think that he had some sort of death wish. You cannot go out there and do whatever you want, no matter who you are.'

John's sister Denise had her own take on events. Since that visit to the Priory, she too had become part of the unfolding story, as she and John had confided in one another. 'The first night they met Michael wanted unprotected sex but John wouldn't do anything with him because, of course, he was HIV positive,' she revealed. 'John didn't tell him that, though. But when Michael confronted him about it in the Priory, John admitted it straight away... Michael just cried when he told him.'

Forty-year-old Denise added that she had had suspicions about her brother's sexuality from a very early age: 'I knew when John was about five or six years old that he was probably gay. John would have nothing to do with boys' toys. It was always dolls that he was interested in. Mum wouldn't buy him dolls, so he'd play with mine instead. I remember he'd smash up his Action Man and Tonka trucks, he didn't want any of them. At that time Mum just put it down to him being brought up by three women – me, my mum and my sister Suzanne. But I always knew because of the way John wanted to try my dresses on. My bras would go missing. At first I'd hunt everywhere for them but eventually I got to realise that I'd find them in his room.

'I was never embarrassed about him being gay,' she continued. 'He's very handsome, and I've lost count of the number of fights I've been in because of him. Women would throw themselves at him and John didn't want to tell them that he was gay because he didn't want to hurt their feelings. So I'd have to go up to them and tell them they were wasting their time.

Denise admitted that it took John a long time to feel able to be open about being gay. 'I think that for a while John tried to lead a normal, straight life because where we're from, Forrest Hall in Newcastle, it was such a big thing, someone being gay,' she said. 'Now it's not such a big deal.'

Yet even though Denise knew John's secret from early on, she only discovered the truth about his HIV infection after he had left the Priory. 'His health has deteriorated already,' she revealed soon after. And, referring to the continuing maelstrom of publicity over Stuart Lubbock's death, she went on: 'All this won't be doing him any good at all. Only this week his face came out in cold sores because of the stress to his weak immune system and he'll need to go to hospital to check his blood count levels. He's still very healthy looking, but that's because he loves going on the sun bed.'

Denise also made it clear that she wasn't exactly a fan of Michael's. 'When I went to the Priory, Barrymore couldn't believe that I wasn't awe-struck and all over him,' she said. 'I got the impression that he's just used to people falling at his feet. When I saw John in the Priory, he just broke down on me. He was in there to help Barrymore but Barrymore still had his bottles of Jack Daniel's in there. And his Valium. I just wish that John had never met Michael Barrymore. John has lost his job as an estate agent and everything because of this.

'I'm so close to John, I feel every bit of hurt he's going through. I know that John would never have brought Barrymore to meet us. We were just too common. John wasn't ashamed of us – it was just [that] Barrymore thought we weren't his kind of people. I think John was just a bit of rough for Barrymore.

'He used to say to John, "I want you to wear this suit because I want you to look like a rent boy,"' Denise revealed. 'He'd dress him in designer suits but John isn't a suit person. He likes to wear jeans and T-shirts.'

Denise is clearly angry by the way she feels her brother was treated by Michael. But John wasn't the only member of her family to be slighted by the celebrity star: 'John loved Barrymore but Barrymore always thought of himself first. When it was Barrymore's birthday, my mum wanted to send him something, but she didn't have much money because she lives off her pension. Yet she still sent him a £40 bunch of flowers, which is a lot of money to her. But he never once rang and thanked my mum. John had to ring her and thank her instead.

'In fact, the first words Barrymore said to my mum were when he and John had popped over to Amsterdam for a break. John was on his mobile to my mum and Barrymore was just full of it. John passed the phone to him and he said, "F***ing hell, not another common Geordie!"

'But my mum wasn't slow off the mark and she wasn't going to take that lying down. She hit back, "I'd rather be a common Geordie than a stinking druggie like you are."'

Denise is scathing about the double-life Michael led during his marriage: 'Barrymore used to say his ex-wife Cheryl was a control freak, but I can't understand how he could be married for nineteen years and then come out and say he was gay.' And she clearly feels that her brother was hurt by what she regards as Michael's sheer arrogance: 'When you meet Barrymore he strips you with his eyes. It's as though he's thinking, Look, I'll talk to you but just remember who I am. But John was so in love with him, he couldn't see him for what he really was.

'None of us was pleased when John told us they were an item,' she added. 'I told him to get out of it. I never even wanted to meet [Barrymore] because I hated the way he belittled ordinary people on his TV shows. That man is a disgrace and has ruined my brother's life.'

John's HIV confession had widespread repercussions. When Michael's previous lover Shaun Davis read reports of the admission in New Zealand he flew back to Britain to discover the truth about exact times and dates. Had Michael been sleeping with John before he split with Shaun?

Speaking at London's Heathrow airport, Shaun would only say tersely: 'Of course I know about the Kenney situation but now isn't the time for me to speak.' He subsequently underwent a blood test and, to his huge relief, it proved negative.

Shaun's mother Christine, who lives in Essex, admitted: 'We all went nutty, really. It was terrible. Shaun came over from New Zealand specifically for the test and is so relieved it has come back negative. Now he has packed his bags and gone back to New Zealand.'

Michael Barrymore was alone. Shaun had left him, John had left him. And he was facing a police death probe. How much worse could it get? He was about to find out...

# 3

# 'HE WAS THRASHING LIKE AN ELECTROCUTED EEL'

JOHN KENNEY wasn't the only witness to the tragic night of the party at Michael's mansion. Two of the guests there that night were Justin Merritt and his sister Kylie. Justin was out for the night with Kylie at the Millennium nightclub when they met Michael Barrymore and their lives, too, changed for ever.

An otherwise unremarkable night was propelled into the extraordinary when one of the club bouncers turned to Justin and remarked: 'We've got a VIP in tonight.' 'Who's that?' asked Justin. 'Michael Barrymore,' replied the bouncer.

Kylie overheard the conversation and could scarcely contain her excitement. She was a huge Barrymore fan and desperately wanted to meet him. So Justin made a fateful decision; his sister would have her wish. 'I decided that we should go over and

44

introduce ourselves,' he said. 'I saw him by the dance floor. He was all over the place, absolutely out of his nut. Loads of people were hanging around him, whispering into his ear and stuff. After we said hello, Barrymore gave Kylie a kiss on the cheek.'

Kylie was delighted, this was turning out to be the night of her life, but Justin could see that Michael was, to put it mildly, overwrought.

He said: 'I looked at him and told him, "You're absolutely ****ed, aren't you?" His face was puffy and he was staggering all over the place. In fact, he looked so out of it I offered to ring him a cab so he could go home.'

But Michael, of course, didn't want the night to end there. He was in party mood. That's when he decided to continue the 'fun' at his mansion. And among those he invited were Justin and Kylie.

As they piled into the taxi at about 2.45 a.m., Justin realised another last-minute guest had climbed into the back seat too… Stuart Lubbock. In the cab, Justin recalled, Michael made a crude joke to the driver. 'The cabbie asked Barrymore if he'd had a good night,' he said. 'And Michael replied, "Yeah, all we need now is a bunk-up." We all laughed but we weren't really sure if he was joking or not.'

Once at the house, Justin Merritt stood open-mouthed at the conspicuous wealth around him. 'In the foyer there's an 8 foot gold statue of an angel perched on a marble stand,' he recalled. 'It's the first thing you see when you walk into his house and it really blew me away. Everything was cream and white, from the marble floor to Regency-style chairs in limed oak. It was very, very expensively decorated. We followed Michael into his kitchen. It is completely state of the art with a gigantic stainless-steel fridge freezer.

'I'm just from a council house and I hadn't been in a mansion like that before,' Justin admitted. He kept saying to us, "What do you want to drink? We've got anything you want", and with a flourish he opened the fridge door to show us bottle after bottle of wine, coolers, spirits, lagers and champagne.

'There were black granite worktops and beautiful cupboards plus every kitchen gadget like coffee machines, blenders and juices. The place reeked of money and good taste.'

Michael Barrymore has strenuously denied Justin's account of what happened next. However, it was then, Justin said, that he sat with Kylie, Stuart Lubbock and Michael around the main worktop in the centre of the kitchen. 'After sorting drinks for everyone, Barrymore produced a small plastic straw and some cocaine wrapped in paper,' he claimed. 'I noticed that it had been ripped from a pornographic magazine.

'He opened the parcel, showed me the coke and asked, "Do you fancy a line?" Then he spread it on the worktop, chopped it up with a credit card and bent down to take a snort with the straw. Michael then offered it to me. I had a line and then he asked Kylie if she wanted one.'

Kylie, nineteen, recalled: 'I said, "No, I'm all right, thanks." I was just trying to take it all in. It was bizarre being in Barrymore's house. We were strangers and he was offering us drugs.'

According to Justin, Michael then turned his attention to Stuart Lubbock, who was drinking a bright red liqueur from a tumbler. 'Michael offered him the coke too,' he added. 'Stuart said, "I'm all right with my Aftershock, thanks."'

It was then, claimed 26-year-old Justin, that Michael dipped his finger into a pile of the powdered drug spread on his kitchen worktop and rubbed it along Stuart's gums. 'I couldn't believe what I was seeing,' Justin added. 'What I saw that night will haunt me for ever.' (While describing Michael's excesses, John Kenney had observed: 'If ever there was a bit of coke powder left over he'd dab it with his finger and rub it on his gums.')

'Stuart jerked his head back as if to say, "What the hell are you doing!" but he didn't try to stop Michael. He was rubbing it on his gums. I was shocked, because I'd never seen that before. I thought you only snorted the stuff.'

Kylie added: 'It seemed such a strange thing to do, sticking his finger in Stuart's mouth.'

Michael would later strenuously deny the cocaine allegations made by Justin and Kylie.

But John wasn't yet at the party and it was in full swing when he arrived home, furious that Michael had left the Millennium club without him. Justin recalled: 'John took Michael aside and they had words. I could tell he was angry that a bunch of strangers were in the house, but I tried to reassure him that everything was OK. Michael put on an Elvis CD and we moved into the lounge where we spread out on one of the three leather sofas. They were a lovely chocolate brown colour. There was a nice happy vibe about the place. I remember there was a model of the Empire State Building which lit up from inside. And in one corner there was a shiny black grand piano.

'Stuart seemed fascinated by everything, star-struck even. There was a cardboard box full of documents and 1920s figurines and Stuart spent ages poring over them. He kept telling Michael what a beautiful place he had and how much he loved it.

'At one point, Stuart asked if I was Michael's bodyguard because I was wearing a white shirt and black trousers. I said I wasn't, but Stuart and I started chatting and soon we realised we both had two kids. He told me his children meant more to him than anything in the world. It was very touching to see a man so fond of his kids. He seemed very sad that he was no longer with their mum and he told me, "It breaks my heart that I can't see them all the time." I felt very sorry for him.'

The conversation drifted and the two men moved to other

parts of the room. Justin started chatting to John Kenney and, he said, they decided to take a dip in the outdoor Jacuzzi. They sat in the warm water, gazing up at the night sky and sipping lagers.

Within minutes, though, they had another sight to occupy them. Stuart Lubbock had rushed out wearing nothing but a pair of dark shorts. 'Stuart seemed hyperactive and very happy,' said Justin. 'He climbed into the Jacuzzi and threw his arms in the air yelling, "Way hey!" as he slid under the water.

'Then he burst up to the surface spluttering water and began giggling hysterically. He kept shouting at me, "Way hey!" and I shouted the same thing back at him. He seemed to be having the time of his life.'

They had been soaking in the hot tub for about ten minutes, said Justin, when Michael strolled outside to check on them. 'I remember him wandering out with a glass of wine in his hand and asking John if he was OK,' he recalled. 'He even put some towelling robes for us by the side of the pool.

'Stuart had a baseball cap in his hand. He threw it into the main pool, got out of the Jacuzzi, then grabbed his knees and dive-bombed into the pool. He was thrashing about in there like an eel [that had] been electrocuted. Michael was just watching with a smile on his face. I was laughing with him too.'

Michael then went back inside the house, Justin recalled. By now the cold was seeping into their bones so he and John decided to go into the house as well.

'I wrapped myself in a robe and went inside,' he said. 'I looked back and there was Stuart on his own in the pool, still larking about in the water. As I walked past the pool to go inside, I put my hand up to Stuart and yelled "Way hey!" and he yelled back. He certainly didn't look to me like he was in trouble, only that he was having a lot of fun.'

Back in Michael's master bedroom, Justin dried off. Now he needed some clothes. He was about to step into the ones he had worn to go to the club when John Kenney gave him yet another insight into a lifestyle where money was no object. 'John opened a cupboard and it was stacked to the brim with brand new T-shirts,' he continued. 'They were white ones from Marks & Spencer. There must have been about a hundred in there.'

John slipped on a T-shirt and sat on the bed, chatting aimlessly to John. He would later estimate that they had been talking for about half an hour when the calm was shattered. 'We were lounging on the bed when there was a commotion,' he said. 'Michael raced into the room, looked past me and said, "John! Someone's floating in the pool!"'

'John and I dashed outside to find Stuart soaking wet and lying on the paving on the right side of the pool near the sun loungers. I don't know who got him out of the water but he was lying there flat on his back with his eyes wide open and the back of his head towards the house. All I saw was his face. [I'd] never seen a dead body before.

'I was desperate to help, so I dialled 999. We didn't know whether Stuart was dead or alive. The operator told me to get Stuart on his side and check if he was breathing. I told John, but he couldn't find a pulse.'

Justin's account of the ensuing events is a little different to the version put forward by John. According to Justin, it was Kylie who gave Stuart the kiss of life. 'Kylie hadn't done life-saving before but she was trying to give him mouth to mouth on my instruction,' Justin explained. 'John crossed his palms over his ribcage and gave him compressions to the chest.'

By now, all the party guests were outside watching Stuart's life ebb away – apart from Michael, whom police later confirmed had run off into the nearby village. Kylie said: 'I didn't know whether I'd get Stuart breathing again. Justin was shouting instructions but John knew what to do anyway. The paramedics arrived and started shocking Stuart with the electrical charger. He still hadn't come around.'

Justin continued: 'The paramedics strapped Stuart to a stretcher and took him out to a waiting ambulance. The garden was suddenly full of police. They asked where Michael was and it was only then that I realised I hadn't seen him since he told us about the body.'

Another party guest, 24-year-old James Futers, would later

tell how he left the bash with a friend and made for his parents' house nearby. 'Michael was completely panic-stricken,' he said. 'He insisted that he'd come with us. He borrowed my mate's mobile phone and I think he was phoning some member of his entourage to ask what he should do. But he was so out of his head he couldn't even dial the number. I remember saying to Michael what a mess we were all in. He just replied, "Why? We didn't kill him." It didn't seem to sink in that a man was lying dead in his property.'

Stuart Lubbock was declared dead at 8.32 a.m. by doctors at Harlow's Princess Alexandra Hospital. By then, an exhausted Justin had gone home to his twelfth-floor council flat in Harlow. Kylie, distressed and tearful, caught a cab back to her mum's.

Justin said: 'The police arrived at my place about twenty minutes later and told me Stuart was dead. I sat there completely stunned. There I was trying to help save this poor lad when it was probably already too late. The police asked me to go through what happened and said they'd be in touch.

'I felt so sorry for Stuart's family, especially his kids. They'd grow up learning that their dad died in a pool during a wild party at a gay comedian's house. What sort of legacy was that to leave behind?'

When John Kenney learned of Justin's insistence that Michael had fed Lubbock cocaine shortly before he drowned, he was stunned. 'For months I haven't known what happened before I arrived at the party,' he told the *News of the World*. 'You don't force drugs on anyone. What was he doing that for? It just proves what kind of man Michael is. I'm glad I'm away from him."

Becoming increasingly bitter towards Michael as he talked, he added: 'I sat around for ages waiting for Michael to come out of the Priory. I was staying with a friend in Hammersmith. In my last call to him he kept saying he missed me, but they were hollow words. I thought, I'm sick of you building me up and then letting me down, so I stopped phoning him. I feel now he used me and dumped me. When the party's going he's great, but when something goes wrong he's a nightmare.'

**4**

# A SHOTGUN IN
# THE DARK

MICHAEL BARRYMORE knew all about nightmares. He had been living in one for as long as he could remember. That night with Stuart Lubbock was the second time he'd stared death in the face... and a life story that disintegrated in a mansion party can be traced back to that first terror when young Michael Barrymore was not yet a teenager.

Huddled beneath the coverlet in a darkened bedroom, the gangly, uncertain boy clutched his mother in terror. He had climbed into her bed to protect her in the bleak council flat that looked out over Bermondsey, south London.

There were always noises, people arguing, people laughing. But this was different and they could both hear it. First came the sound of footsteps on the concrete stairs outside their council flat, then the creak that was the front door opening.

A draught of night air blew through the hallway and chilled the slick of perspiration on his forehead. The hall light was on and the shadow that fell across the carpet clearly identified the man in the passageway. It was his wife-beating brute of a father, lurching home after yet another night out gambling away what little money they had.

A friend of Michael's, who knows the torment he endured during those early years revealed: 'Michael's dad burst into the room and pointed this shotgun at them both. Michael told me he remembers it waving around, back and fore, between them both. Then, without so much as a word, his dad puts the gun down, backs away from the door and disappears. Gone for good! Neither Michael nor his mother ever saw him again. Of course, they didn't know that at the time, they just lay there in bed, holding each other and waiting for him to come back with the gun.'

Michael admitted: 'The way he treated my mother and the dreadful things I saw when I was a child have stayed in my mind forever. I know one thing – I'll never, ever gamble. People don't understand how bad compulsive gambling is. My mother used to say that she'd rather my father were an alcoholic than a gambler, because at least there's a limit to how much someone can drink, whereas gambling just goes on and on. Even the savings out of my money box used to go.'

But this was no giant hulk of thug. Michael's father ruled by fear. 'I remember him as a dapper man, charming when he was sober,' the celebrity remembered in later life. 'He looked a bit like David Niven, very sharp and clean. He had Brylcreemed hair, shoes you could see your face in. And he lost money on the horses.'

It would be years before that little boy in the bed would change his name to Barrymore in deference to his film heroes Lionel and John Barrymore. He was born Michael Kieran Parker on May 4, 1952 in Bermondsey. And the entertainment world he would come to dominate was very different then from the way it is today. The big movies of 1952 were *High Noon* and *Singin' in the Rain*. There wasn't much singing in the flat where young Michael grew up. Plenty of rain though, as he stepped out of the front door and, when he was big enough, peered over the concrete balcony of the shared landing to the council estate beyond. And then there was that sound – the crunch of feet on stairs as his dad came home to give his mother another beating.

There were already two children in the house – John and Anne – when baby Michael came along. He wasn't planned. Another mouth to feed, another demand on mum Margaret's already overstretched purse strings. Less money for his dad to gamble. By the time Michael was six he was painfully aware that this was not a happy home. Brother John was a lot older and he was out a lot. Sister Anne suffered from polio, so she was in hospital much of the time. That left Michael on his own to bear the brunt of the arguing around him.

Day after day he would trudge to school, first St Joseph's Primary, then St Michael's Roman Catholic Secondary, aching for the normal, loving life he thought his friends were leading. Then he'd come home to a nightmare. A neighbour recalled 'There was a lot of screaming when we passed. Terrible shouting. Once or twice Michael would run out and stand on the stairs just to get away from it. It was pitiful to see him.'

Michael was about eight when he underwent one of the defining experiences of his life. In an episode that might have brought a brief moment of respite to his mother, his dad came home drunk but this time he fell down in a stupor in the hallway before he had a chance to become violent. The little change that he had left fell out of his pocket and rolled along the floor. Michael and his brother grabbed it, ran down the stairs and counted it. There was enough to get them into the cinema at the Elephant and Castle. There was a Norman Wisdom film on, called *Trouble in Store*. As the film played, Michael watched the audience as much as he watched the film. People were laughing out loud, having the time of their lives. And in a flash of inspiration he knew what he wanted to do more than anything else in life. He wanted to make people laugh like Norman did.

'I remember that film well,' recalled Michael with a smile. 'It was the first film I'd ever seen. He made me forget about the problems at home, problems with my father. Even at that age, I realised you could be taken out of yourself by comedy.'

Brother John confirmed the effect that the film had on the future TV celebrity: 'After that, Michael followed me everywhere, always doing funny voices and saying that he was going to become a star.' The seeds of his future had been sown. 'We'd be watching TV and I used to send things up,' Michael remembered. '*Sale of the Century* would be on, for example, and I'd make little comments or answer totally different questions. People would giggle and that gave me the confidence to carry on joking.'

Showbiz wasn't the most straightforward ambition for a young boy, but early on Michael had learned the value of working hard to earn a living. His mum would often do more than one job to make ends meet. And when his father left he was determined to assume responsibility for his mum.

'It was that toughness of my childhood that made me what I am today,' said Michael. 'It gave me the edge you need to make it in this business. I remember that at first, when my dad had just left, I used to make excuses that he was a long-distance lorry driver to save face. And at school I discovered that if you were a good fighter or you could entertain people, you survived. So I entertained. Nobody asks awkward questions, like "Where's your dad?", when they're laughing.

'But though I knew I wanted to end up on stage, it was considered sissy even to do amateur dramatics at our school. The only reason I got parts was because nobody else would get up on the stage and suddenly all the teachers liked me. I thought, this ain't a bad game, is it? One minute I'm getting the cane, the next minute the English teacher is praising me.'

Eventually Michael – by now known as 'Bones' Parker, the biggest mimic around – gained the confidence to admit that his dad had gone. He explained with a wry smile: 'Mates from school would come around and if they wanted a sandwich, I'd say, "OK, that'll be half a crown." If they moaned, I'd say, "You've got to pay, you've got a dad, I haven't."'

But for all his enthusiasm, by the age of fifteen Michael still hadn't worked out how to make the jump from Bermondsey to the stage. He needed a springboard and he needed to be noticed. And in the Swinging Sixties there was one place where you could guarantee a regular supply of stars and showbiz agents – all unable to move from their seats for the best part of an hour while you gave them your all... the studios of hairstylist Vidal Sassoon.

With little idea of how to tell one end of a pair of scissors from another, Michael went for it. 'All my mates were working on the docks or in local firms,' he shrugged. 'I didn't want to be a hairdresser, but because stars went to Vidal's, I thought maybe I'd get a break that way. It was terrible logic.

'I thought I could perform for big names when they came in. I was fifteen and used to do Shirley Bassey impressions for Candice Bergen and all that. By laughter, I learned that you can win people over. Mind you, Shirley Bassey didn't like being called Shirl; still, that's what I used to call her. But I gave up the hairdressing when I realised it was going nowhere. I was only on £3.50 a week and earned more in tips.'

**5**

# THEY CALL HIM THE HIM THE PILL TESTER

DOING IMPRESSIONS of Shirley Bassey amongst the curlers, sprays and stylists of Vidal Sassoon was one thing. Getting from there to the top of the entertainment tree was quite another. But at sixteen Michael saw a five-strong band of youngsters his own age playing pop music at a club near his home and a new idea dawned on him. This is it, he thought, I'm going to be a musician.

Michael was determined to join the group, known as The New Look Soul Band. There was just one small problem: he couldn't play a note on anything. Undaunted, he persuaded his mother to buy him an electric organ and started taking keyboard lessons. Meanwhile, he hung around whenever the boys were playing.

Soon Michael was on first-name terms with singer and drummer John Moore, lead guitarist Peter Outram, rhythm guitarist and electric organist Peter Doran and bass guitarist Alan Shephard.

When Peter Doran left the band to take up a university place, Michael was in like greased lightning. 'The reason I got in was that I was the only person they knew who had his own keyboard,' he grinned. 'I had hair like a Yeti, I wore an old Army trenchcoat and green crushed velvet trousers. It was a great experience.'

But even in the framework of a music group, Michael couldn't resist using his comic gift. At the drop of a hat he'd do impressions of Ken Dodd, Mick Jagger, Alan Whicker, Frankie Howerd, Albert Steptoe and Bernie Winters. A pal of his at the time remembered: 'Everywhere we went he'd end up jumping on a table and doing his impersonations. He loved the attention. He even used to carry a rolled-up fez in the back of his trousers so he could take off Tommy Cooper.' Michael himself admitted: 'I used to stand on my head holding the notes. I was c\*\*p, but I was good visually.'

At first the band took its 'progressive rock' sounds to pubs and clubs around London. But by 1969 they went international and secured a two-week contract in Germany – the only problem being, they didn't have a van to carry their gear. Michael's mum Margaret came to the rescue again. She took out a £3,000 loan so they could make the gig. They went to

Germany and did five-hour sets in a strip club. Michael fondly recalled, 'It was a great experience.'

Though it might have seemed like five hours, in fact the band played six 45-minute sessions each night between 8 p.m. and 4 a.m. Six days a week. The audiences loved them. Backstage, though, Michael was sowing the seeds of his future downfall. Hangers-on would be drawn to his personality, he would latch on to anyone with a friendly face – and that's how he became a guinea pig for drugs.

'Most of the people in the clubs liked the odd joint, though I don't think Micky was into wacky-baccy,' Michael's pal told the *Daily Mirror*. 'He used to say it didn't do much for him. But he did try out pills for other people to see what effect they had. They used to call him the Pill Tester.'

He was also making a good job of being heterosexual. At one stage the boys were performing at the K52 Club in Frankfurt and living in a room with six bunk beds and a bathroom. By about 2 a.m. Michael had chatted up a groupie he had met backstage. He brought her back to the communal room, wriggled under a pile of blankets with her and had sex while the rest of his pals were trying to concentrate on their card game a few feet away.

From Germany, the band went on to St Gallen in Switzerland, where they had managed to get a two-month residency at a club called the Africana. The boys had been given a place to sleep above a shop on the high street.

It was too much to expect them to stay out of trouble. There was a flagpole with the Swiss national banner just below the window – and, worryingly, just within reach. One night, the boys swapped it for Michael's boxer shorts 'for a laugh', not counting on the locals becoming very upset the following morning. Within hours, in a flashback to the darkest hours of his childhood, Michael found himself staring down the barrel of a gun once more as armed cops burst into the room. The band was arrested for debasing the Swiss national flag, though officers eventually settled for a grovelling apology.

In the spring of 1970, the lads returned home and changed their name to Fine China, but after a year of trying to make it big in Britain, they broke up. Michael was eighteen, just. So he took a chance and applied for a job as a Butlin's Redcoat. The normal minimum age for entry at the time was twenty-one, so Michael took the only route open to him... he lied. At least he did it in a good voice. 'I was going to speech therapy classes in the evenings,' he confessed. 'You see, my Bermondsey accent was so thick that people literally couldn't understand a word I said.'

Despite the rock and pop revolution of the mid-Sixties, Des O'Connor and Ken Dodd were among the kings of TV and light entertainment for much of the decade. A spot on the Royal Command Performance was still one of the pinnacles of a showbiz career and being a Redcoat was the accepted bottom rung on the ladder.

Many of those who worked with Michael recall a man who worked hard to make it, even if some of them never thought he would. Of course, those former colleagues from Butlin's remember him as Mike Parker, the man who was 'all arms and legs', a trait that would become a trademark of his work.

Mike Onions was the camp compere at Clacton. In an interview with the *Daily Mail*, he revealed, 'I was producer of the Redcoat show. Janet, my wife choreographed a dance routine – 'The Rhythm of Life' from *Sweet Charity* – for the Redcoats, but Michael wasn't particularly good. He was all arms and legs. My main claim to fame came when the entertainments manager Mr Brigden was looking for someone to support the late-night cabaret stars who performed in one of the bars. We had some really big names – Diana Dors, Matt Monro, Hughie Green and the Barron Knights.'

Mr Onions continued: 'Michael was the only one who had an act of any sort, so he was called in to the office for an audition. He did impressions, but he was very, very raw. Afterwards, Mr Brigden called me in and said, "Michael's not good enough. You'll have to do it." So I ended up supporting some of the biggest names in show business. I also remember that Mike used to ride "the largest donkey in the world", because with his long legs, he was the least likely to fall off.

Maybe that's why he has never spoken to me since! But I think he probably learned a great deal from being in the Redcoat show. When I look at his work, I can't help feeling a lot of it is pure holiday camp. Mike is still using the basics we worked out all those years ago.'

Mavis Jones was the chief Redcoat at that Butlin's. 'Michael used to help me on Friday afternoons when I gave out the raffle prizes,' she told the *Daily Mail*. 'Unfortunately I had been left with the stock from the year before, which was completely unsuitable. I got quite upset about it and I remember Michael coming over, putting his arm around me, leaning his head on my shoulder and saying "Awight!", just like he does on television. He was always very caring.

'He never excelled with his own age group. He was always much better with people who were a bit older and who appreciated it when he took the mickey out of them. I think his contemporaries took themselves a bit too seriously. One of his favourite tricks was to pick people up suddenly and fling them round in a circle. I was watching him on television recently and thought how little he has changed. Even then he had the same characteristic walk, always looking down at his feet. Before I knew who Mike Parker became, I'd seen Barrymore many times on television and I'd said to my husband, "I'm sure I know that lad from somewhere." It wasn't the way he looked that was so familiar, but the characteristics.'

After Butlin's, Michael tried other holiday camp jobs, such as entertaining kids at Norton Park Holiday camp in Dartmouth, Devon. It was here he saved a boy from drowning when he was playing Cowboys and Indians with children near the swimming pool.

As five-year-old Scunthorpe lad Gordon Mann stood laughing at the water's edge another boy pushed him in for a joke. 'All I can remember is plunging into the pool, my toes touching the bottom and the feeling of sinking,' said Gordon, recalling the incident years later, 'I couldn't swim and I was desperately trying to get to the surface. Then Michael caught hold of me. I'm so grateful. Michael saved my life when he dragged me out. I'd have drowned if he hadn't been there. Afterwards he came to see me and bought me a Tonka toy truck.' Gordon said that he'd be grateful to Michael for the rest of his life.

With his holiday camp career behind him, Michael flirted with the idea of drama school so he could get into acting, as his hero Norman Wisdom had done. He even gained a scholarship. 'Then, just before I was due to go, I won a talent contest in a pub as a comic,' he said. 'I only won because all my mates were in the audience, but I threw up the chance of drama school and went on the road as a comic.' Unfortunately, his decision backfired: 'I had a rubbish act and got paid off at every place I appeared. Suddenly I was out of work and forced to drive a lorry at Covent Garden for a living.'

From there he moved on to a different kind of driving and became a chauffeur to the head of Sainsbury's. His brother John recalled: 'He used to clean the governor's car and drive him around. It was a superb hand-built Bristol, very expensive and fast, but Michael had the confidence to drive it.' Barry Mulligan, who became the comic's best friend and manager, added: 'Michael used to say, "I'll have one of these one day." He used to park it outside his mum's and take his mates for a ride around the block in it.'

The route to actually getting a limousine of his own came when Michael least expected it, and to begin with he was absolutely dead set against the idea: '*New Faces*? A talent show? You'll never get me on that. Look at the panel of judges. They're hard, they are. Why would I want to put myself through that?' How could he have known that this was the show that would be his springboard to fame and fortune – and bring him to the brink of destruction in the process?

By now it was the mid-Seventies. Michael had a friend called Jack Louis who was desperate to make it big on TV. There was a New Faces audition in Bristol. 'Will you come with me?' Jack asked Michael. 'Bit of moral support?'

At the time, Michael reckoned his club act was coming on a bit, and he was earning up to £100 a week. But he wasn't going to let down a friend, so he and Jack made their way to Bristol and dutifully waited in line. Jack was handed a form to fill in and, before he knew it, Michael got one too. 'No,' he said, pointing at Jack. 'Not for me. I'm only here with him.' But the production worker was insistent. 'You might as well have one,' he was told.

'I was an insecure kid, green as anything,' said Michael. 'They pressured me to fill in that form, so I filled in someone else's name, and with a different address and somebody else's telephone number. You see, I've never pushed myself, I've always needed someone to make decisions for me. If I'm out there on stage, I'll go for it, but you've got to push me. Anyway, I did the audition.'

He stood on his head and did an impression of an Australian. From the incredulous looks on the faces of the audience, he was certain that he'd died a death. 'Then, two weeks later, a researcher tracked me down to my digs – I don't know how – and said they wanted me on in a fortnight's time,' he remembered. 'I told her, "Nah, I don't want to do it." But she persisted. So I asked her, "What would you do if you were me?" She answered, "What have you got to lose?" So a fortnight later I won it.' In fact, he was a *New Faces* sensation, scoring ninety-five out of a possible one hundred points, plus the viewers' vote.

The publicity brought work, though it was still lower-league stuff. First came a stint at a club called the Showboat in London's Strand, then a summer season with the Black and

White Minstrels. Michael was bottom of the bill with a ten-minute slot.

This was a golden period in his life. He was doing what he loved best and he was becoming more successful by the week. What mattered to him more than anything was the audience, and that feeling that rushed through him every time he stepped out on stage and heard those first peals of laughter. 'I was so determined it was frightening,' he remembered. And that determination even helped him overcome the nights when there was no laughter at all!

His TV break had been a start, but there was still a lot of work to do. 'I was discovering that three minutes on *New Faces* does not make a career,' he smiled. 'One night I was booked to play this club in Doncaster with a 2,000 capacity. Sixteen people were in – I counted them. I could hear my words echoing round the place. I got so terrified my tongue started to stick to the roof of my mouth. Eventually I was talking rubbish. I walked off to complete silence. Later I found out the sixteen were all Belgians who didn't speak a word of English.'

# 6

# 'IF I HADN'T ABANDONED MY MUM, I'D HAVE LOST MY WIFE'

IT WAS back at the Showboat in London's Strand that Michael had performed his most astute engagement... he'd met a heart-stoppingly pretty singer and dancer called Cheryl St Clair. Well, that was her stage name. Her maiden name was Cocklin. She was a divorcee and her previous husband was film producer Greg Smith.

Besides Michael, there were two other comedians and a dance troupe on the bill. The producer thought the show was a little unbalanced and needed a singer. That's where Cheryl came in. She had her own dressing room a floor above Michael's, which was in the basement. One night Michael was sitting in his room, going over his act in his mind, when there was a knock. A tousle of red hair peered around the door. Racked with insecurity, he was half expecting her to tell him what was wrong with his act, how he should be more mainstream if he was ever going to get on TV with any regularity.

Beneath the red hair were the brightest eyes he'd ever encountered, and a smile that could light Blackpool. 'You know,' the newcomer said, her smile broadening. 'I think you're the best thing I've ever seen.' Michael was bowled over. Not just because of the way she looked – there were already stirrings within him that made a woman's looks less important to him than to many men. But this woman, he realised, knew people in TV. Her opinion mattered.

Cheryl became his first serious girlfriend. And in the glow of happiness that enveloped him, Michael pushed to the deepest recesses of his mind the demons that had beset him for years. The torment that would take over and transform his life beyond all recognition. The struggle with his own sexuality.

Cheryl's version of her first meeting with Michael is fascinating to hear. 'I first saw him in a London club,' she explained. 'The reviews had been awful. He came on after the dancers – all teeth, long hair and check suit. I thought sarcastically, "This is going to be good." Then I saw him perform. He knocked me and the audience dead. I'd never managed anyone before, but I promised Michael I'd work for him until I dropped. We pooled our money, got his teeth fixed and I took care of his presentation, particularly his wardrobe. He looked like a clown. When I first saw his act he'd worn his check suit, did a sketch with a box over his head, dropped his trousers and carried a woman off stage. When I changed his stage clothes, the effect was dramatic. He looked sophisticated and worked better than he had ever worked before.'

At first, though Michael was falling in love, Cheryl saw it as a purely business relationship. Then she was involved in a terrible car smash. 'I'd been divorced for six years and had no intention of marrying again,' she explained. 'But three months after our first meeting I was badly shaken up when a car crashed into my Mini. The only person I wanted was Michael. That made me realise I was falling head over heels in love.'

Michael certainly understood the head over heels bit. By 1976, he was regularly performing impressions while standing on his head. 'It started when I began taking off Australians,' he said that same year. 'I did the *New Faces* audition, then I progressed to Alan Whicker sending a story from Down Under. I gesticulated with my legs instead of my arms. It's not easy, I can tell you. But it seems to go down well in the clubs where I perform.'

Isn't it painful? Michael was asked at the time. 'I think it's good for you,' he replied. 'If I'm dead in five years' time, I'll know I was wrong. It makes my shoulders ache and I think I'm getting a small bald patch just where I rest my head on the floor. Otherwise I seem to be fine.' The audiences certainly liked it: Michael went on to make his first appearance on the television show *Now Who Do You Do*, on which he impersonated, amongst others, John Wayne and Fanny Craddock. The audience lapped it up. The effect, said one commentator, was that of a dying spider with a rapid line in patter.

Getting married to Cheryl also seemed a good idea at the time. How better to stop those 'forbidden' urges that plagued him at unbidden moments? Urges that would never go away, no matter how hard he tried to banish them. 'I was always conscious that I like being with blokes,' Michael now admits. 'I didn't propose to Cheryl thinking, Oh, this'll make me straight. But my subconscious was probably going, Well, this'll get rid of that. In retrospect, proposing to her was rash.

'Even when I started going out with Cheryl I'd had struggles with my sexuality,' he continues. 'It came up when I was a child, and when I was in my teens. But you don't put your hand up and say, 'I think I've got a problem'. I couldn't even say the word "gay". It would choke in my throat.'

Looking back on that time, a friend explained: 'Until now, he hadn't put himself in positions where he'd had a permanent girlfriend. There had been the pop band tour abroad, but then it was just a series of one-night stands, and there was that hilarious story in his autobiography about his first sexual encounter with a girl up against her bedroom door. He said something like, "She's screaming, I think I'm giving her pleasure, but I was doing it to the gap in the door."

'But now Cheryl was on the scene, things were different. If he hoped his homosexual leanings were a phase that he'd grow out of, now was the time to put those leanings well and truly to rest.

'Michael told me that he proposed to Cheryl in the front room of her mum and dad's house. She thought he was having her on, but eventually he convinced her he was serious and she went and told her parents. Apparently, they weren't too happy about it.'

They married on June 10, 1976 at Epping Register Office. Cheryl looked sensational in white and Michael wore a dark suit and a loud, striped tie. The pair looked a picture of happiness as they cut the two-tiered wedding cake.

But as Mrs Barrymore, Cheryl was going to have to get used to precious little cake and small portions of everything else, at least in the short term. Her first priority was to get some money into the new household. 'We were so broke that Michael got a job in Selfridges and some rare cabaret work in the evening,' she recalled. 'I worked in a dress shop in Golders Green. For all my faith in his talent we were on the verge of giving up.'

Then Michael got another break, a spot on *The Little and*

*Large Show* in Bournemouth. 'Michael was at the bottom of the bill,' said Cheryl. 'He went on first and was so good I felt sorry for anyone going on after him. There were important producers in the audience, and that night he was given a big contract and never really looked back.'

Soon afterwards, as the money began to roll in, Michael confessed: 'I owe it all to Cheryl. I don't know where I'd be without her. I need a strong woman and Cheryl's certainly that. We're best friends, best mates, whichever is the greater. I've never been happier. There'll be good times, bad times and dull times, but we'll survive. I don't mind facing an audience of thousands, but I get shy meeting a few people in a room. I'm a long way from the mad extrovert you see on stage.'

But in the same year that they got married, just when Michael was beginning to find some showbiz success, he made one of his greatest mistakes and invested in a business for his family. To be fair, it all started out so well. Michael paid a deposit on a newsagents and sweetshop in Bermondsey and got his brother John to manage it. The shop had done well under its previous owners, so Michael reckoned that, if all else went wrong in his life, at least this would act as a bit of insurance.

John moved into the flat above the house and they all set to work. Michael recalled: 'Cheryl and I used to serve sweets and we were in competition with a bloke a couple of doors up. So

I'd have a laugh with local kids, make them giggle and they'd come in to our shop and ignore the other fella. When I was a kid, making people laugh was a defence mechanism. It also worked with grown-ups. Sample comedy line to adults: "I'm half Irish. Got any Irish in you, luv? Would you like some?"'

Then the rot set in. Brother John explained: 'When we bought the lease on the shop in Bermondsey we called it The Parker Brothers. Michael put up the £1,000 deposit, but me and my wife Carmel ran it day in, day out, seven days a week. I used to send Michael £100 a week from the takings. But after a few months Michael said to me, "I've got a summer season coming up and I'm doing great. So you can have the shop." Then Cheryl turned up. Cheryl said things hadn't gone as well as they'd thought and wanted some of the shop's takings. But I was in a bit of a mess at the time, I owed some money on some of the stock, and my wife hit the roof. The two of them went at it like cats in the street. They were slagging each other off something rotten. Cheryl was screaming, "We want no more to do with you." Then the shop went bust.'

Michael's version of events is a little different. He poured his heart out to a showbiz pal as his world crumbled around him, and that pal later revealed Michael's side of the story: 'When Michael came back from summer season he was knackered. He gives his all when he's on stage and hadn't really bothered with anything else, so he was surprised to walk into the shop and see his mum there by herself. Apparently, his brother was out of the country. I think Michael said something about Ireland.

'Anyway, Michael called the accountants in to see what was going on and it was only then, he said, that the full extent of the problem was put in front if him. He told me that he was made bankrupt with a debt of around £40,000.'

It's a large amount now. Back then it was astronomical. It meant that Michael and Cheryl lost virtually all they had, though at least they kept their flat because it was rented from the council. Cheryl's dad Eddie had to help them with cash handouts. Immensely grateful, Michael came to look upon him as his own father, replacing the one who had walked out on him all those years ago. But the worst legacy of those days was that the family row that followed the shop's closure wrecked Michael's relationship with his brother and, ultimately, with his mother.

All communication with John stopped virtually immediately, but bit by bit, Michael stopped talking to his mother too. The disintegration of their old closeness was a long, long process. Cheryl blamed Michael's family for putting them in this situation. Michael wasn't so set in his opinions, but ended up siding with his wife.

'I was a registered bankrupt for five years,' he admits now. 'If you're made personally bankrupt they're allowed to take everything away from you, or they were then. They may not have been able to take my flat but all that was left was a mattress, one change of clothes and our wedding rings and that was it. Without a subsidy from Eddie we wouldn't have survived.'

But the price to pay over the failed business enterprise was a heavy one. 'It split the family apart totally,' Michael confesses. 'I tried to make excuses for them, saying it might have been this and it might have been that, but Cheryl wasn't happy. "How could your family do that to you?" she kept asking. She said my mum must have known what was going on and should have told me.

'First of all there was absolutely no communication whatsoever with my brother and then, finally, with my mum. With the benefit of hindsight, Michael feels that he should have behaved differently. 'I should have stood up for myself and said, "I don't think my mum is to blame, I don't want to drag her into this." But Cheryl didn't want me to have anything to do with the family.'

'If Cheryl hadn't been so dogmatic,' he added, 'it would have been resolved much earlier. When we eventually stopped talking I didn't speak to Mum again for about eight years. But I believed at the time, quite without any doubt whatsoever, that if I hadn't abandoned my mum and my family I'd have been abandoned by my wife.'

With Cheryl still behind him, Michael threw himself heart and soul into building his continuing showbiz reputation and restoring his bank balance. Even so, life wasn't easy for a comparatively little-known entertainer and that all important big television contract was still some way off.

By 1979, he was still only the bottom of the bill at a summer show in Great Yarmouth. A year later the summer show was in the Winter Gardens Theatre, Bournemouth, and he had edged only slightly further up the bill. The act was coming along, though. Halfway through, Michael had taken to whipping a black beret out of his pocket, announcing: 'Impersonation of Chuck Berry' and flinging the beret across the stage. At another point, he'd invite a member of the audience to help him in his rendition of *Swan Lake*. It consisted of Michael putting on a swan mask, which he then got tangled up in his helper's legs. As the laughter grew, so did his confidence – not least, according to one interviewer in the *Daily Mirror*, because of a 'defiance born out of desperation'. 'Since you saw me last year it's been the longest twelve months of my life,' Michael told the *Mail*. 'We were certain it was all going to happen. Producers from all the TV channels came to see the show and said they had great plans for me. But nothing came of it and I'm still more or less at the bottom of the bill. My act is better and longer and I'm in a better class of show. To be original and fairly unknown can be a difficult thing. I sometimes feel as if fame is just another rung, another step away.'

Was he simply too good looking to be a comedian? asked the interviewer with a smile. 'Maybe I could get plastic surgery to make me all ugly,' Michael joked back. 'Throw myself at a brick wall, flatten my nose, redden it up, wear baggy pants. But that wouldn't be me. At one time I was so worked up about being a success I used to sit up in bed and do my whole act in my sleep. Those days have gone now. I'm tougher and wiser and a long, long year older. I feel a lot older than my late twenties. You know, what I don't want is to finish up a failure with no dignity. If I'm going to fail, I want to do it with dignity and style.'

In 1981 he climbed the next rung of the entertainment ladder, securing a spot on TV hit show *The Russ Abbott Saturday Madhouse*. It was on this show that he created the characters of Gordon Bluey and the Weathermen. By now, Michael was able to appreciate that the long road to success had been an invaluable training for him. The fact that he had fallen flat on his face at a number of club bookings had helped him learn how to keep an audience really entertained. 'I was a disaster,' he admitted. 'They paid me off after the first night at every one of those clubs!' It wasn't an experience he would have to undergo again – but neither was it an experience he forgot. 'They were really tough days,' Michael said, 'and I really thought I was nearing the end.'

Russ Abbot was Michael's turning point. 'As a virtually

inexperienced performer, I thought it was fantastic that I was asked to join the team,' he said. 'It certainly helped me to develop, to relate to an audience and learn about the workings of television. Russ Abbot was marvellous, too, and very generous in letting me and the other "inmates" of the Madhouse have a fair share of the limelight.'

John Fisher, who gave Michael his first break on the BBC, was clearly impressed by the new comedian. 'I saw something very special,' he remembered, 'a creative spontaneity, something one hasn't really seen since Danny Kaye, the ability to be in charge of 3,000 people.'

Michael's appearances on Russ Abbot's show were extremely successful. He was also slowly moving up that all-important billing when it came to variety shows, sharing third place with a musical puppet act called Pepe and his Friends, just above Johnny Hutch and the Half Wits. And all the time the act was progressing. Michael had added John Cleese-style walks to the repertoire and was teasing his audience more than ever. When he spotted girls going to the loo, he would bound from the stage, chase after his victim, drag her out of the ladies and up on to stage, where he'd proclaim: 'Give this girl a potty!' The unfortunate victim would cringe with embarrassment, Michael would be triumphant and the audience, brought up on toilet jokes that the non-British never really understand, were in stitches.

On the subject of his manic energy, Michael once explained: 'When a performance is over, my body feels like a steamroller's gone over it. But one of the reasons I work like I do is [because] when I stop, then what do I do? What happens then? I just keep myself busy. You get such an adrenalin rush when you're working. My favourite part is rehearsals, the build-up. It's like the run-up to Christmas – it's great when it happens and it's a big letdown when the day's all gone.

'I don't know if the way I work comes from years of having nothing. I think it's that I don't ever take anything for granted or assume the audience know me so I can take it easy – because that's the shortest route to losing everything.'

Michael's public profile was beginning to grow. He started popping up on Little and Large's TV show and *Blankety Blank*. Then, in 1982, he finally got what he had always wanted: a television series of his own. It was to be made in November and screened the following year. Philip Jones, the boss of Thames Television, had seen Michael guesting on the mime show *Give Us A Clue* and was impressed: 'Michael has a slightly abrasive edge to him,' he said at the time. 'He can get quite tough with an audience, the way Bruce Forsyth can. I really believe in him as a face of the future.' Michael was delighted, but modest about his success. 'It's taken me eleven years – but you have to mature as a comedian,' he said. 'At nineteen it didn't work for me to tell gags about the family – I didn't have enough lines on my face. But things are coming along nicely now. After all, if I'd been a footballer I'd be facing up to the end of my career by now.'

The series, called *The Michael Barrymore Show*, was an immediate success. Michael was catapulted in to the stardom he had always yearned for, but he didn't let it go to his head. Rather, he won his colleagues' admiration and affection. The dance group Bunch of Five appeared on the show and became immediate fans: 'Michael is so good when he dances with us that I'd like to call us the Bunch of Six,' said dance troupe member Paul Hillier. 'And Michael doesn't behave like a megastar. So many dancers are treated as back-ups to someone's act, not as performers in their own right. I don't think Michael has done much dancing before, but he's really worked hard to perfect routines with us. We had to teach him to cartwheel, and that isn't easy, when you're over 6 foot, like he is. It took him two weeks' extra rehearsal and a lot of bruises, but he now does it as well as us.'

The audiences loved him, not least because he treated them with an amused irreverence they found irresistible. 'Clear orf,' he growled at the end of the last show of the series. They did so, cheering and laughing.

Another key to Michael's success was that he took in everything around him, right from the early days. Larry Grayson had helped the younger comedian in this respect, taking him to one side and telling him: 'When you're not on stage, keep your mouth shut and your ears open.'

In 1983 Michael got the ultimate showbiz reward, a spot on the Royal Variety Show. It was a huge success and brought more praise from his colleagues: 'I got on really well with Michael when we did the Royal Variety together,' said Jason Donovan, a huge star at the time. 'We had a good laugh backstage. He's even funnier on real life than he is on TV.'

Michael did the dying swan in *Swan Lake* again, this time accompanied by a fishmonger's wife he picked from the audience. It brought the house down and introduced Michael to royalty. 'All I can remember about meeting the Queen afterwards was feeling desperately nervous as she got nearer and nearer down the line of people who were being presented to her,' he remembered. 'And I can also remember Billy Dainty calling out to me, "Tell her how you did in Yarmouth." Billy had seen me die a death in Yarmouth a few years before. But I was thrilled when the Queen told me she'd enjoyed the dancing part of my act.'

Next, Michael took to banishing members of the audience from the theatre, which, if anything, made him even more popular with his adoring fans. 'I can only be like that on stage in front of hundreds of people,' he confessed, a sentiment shared by millions of entertainers whose extrovert on-stage personality may be very different from the person they are in everyday life. 'Off stage I'm really quiet and shy and there are times when I'm dead scared one of my victims will turn around and bash me one.'

The first series of *The Michael Barrymore Show* had been such a success that Michael was immediately signed up for another. He and Cheryl were delighted: they were determined to improve their flat in Harlow, Essex and enjoy the trappings of their new-found success. But they weren't going to go too wild: all those years of struggle had taught them to be cautious.

'Success means I can give Cheryl all the good things that my mother never had,' Michael revealed during the first flush of his celebrity success. 'But I'm not really materialistic. We're having our flat in Essex done up, but I'm not going to go mad and buy a big house in London and a Rolls-Royce. This is a dodgy business and suddenly your success can vanish.'

That said, however, success was definitely beginning to change Michael's life. 'Since I've had my own TV series, I've started being recognised,' he admitted. 'I have to add an hour to my shopping time in Tesco.'

Now that Michael had finally become a hot property, the public couldn't get enough of him. That Christmas he appeared in panto in Wolverhampton and promptly ushered in the New Year hosting the TV show, *At Last – It's 1984*. He then went on to host a trial comeback of the show *Beat the Clock*, which brought a compliment from one of the show's original hosts,

Bob Monkhouse – although Michael was later to fall out massively with him. 'Michael is perfect for Beat the Clock. I hope it takes off,' said Bob. 'He has that right manner, that ruthless manipulation of the public, a bit like the old Brucie.'

That year also saw Michael hosting the panel game *Get Set Go!* – and it was a mark of quite how quickly he'd risen, and how highly, that there were complaints the show was too mundane for his talents. It lasted for just one series. But the loss of that show wasn't likely to affect the momentum of Michael Barrymore's career now. He was on a roll, being compared with John Cleese, Freddie Starr and, oddly, Max Bygraves. But he refused to take his new life for granted.

In one interview of the time, Michael revealed something about the preparation for his shows, preparation much influenced by the fact that they now contained so much audience participation. 'Before the start of each programme, the producer and I stand up in the balconies and watch the public come in,' he explained. 'It's then that we pick suitable candidates to take part in the show. We keep a firm eye on them and make sure they are sitting in accessible seats! It's difficult to say how we can tell who'll be good for a laugh – it's just intuition really, and we usually make the right choice.'

And Michael denied that he hurt those who joined him on stage. 'I'm not nasty,' he argued. 'Some comics pick on someone's looks or clothes and continuously knock them for the fun of it. I don't do that. I prefer to have fun with a member of the audience rather than at them. If someone really didn't want to come up on stage, I'd leave them alone and choose another. What I really like about involving the audience is that each person behaves differently. So, even if you're doing the same act as the night before – as you do in clubs – it's never going to be exactly the same. I have to do a lot of ad-libbing.'

That said, the audience had generally come to know what to expect. 'There's always an element of danger for anyone who comes to watch me,' Michael said soon afterwards. 'They never know what I'm going to do or who I'll pick on. I don't think I really slag off my audience, but I do use people as my stooges to get laughs.' It was, however, a two-way process, as Michael revealed: 'People will write in saying, "I'll be sitting in row so-and-so and I'd like you to throw out my husband – he has a moustache and glasses… "'

Along with Anneka Rice, Michael was voted Rear Of The Year in 1986: he rose to the occasion and shared his thoughts with the nation. 'I was astounded because I never thought anyone noticed my backside – I move about so fast,' he said. 'In fact, I haven't got a bum, it's completely flat. When it comes to underwear, I'm totally hooked on a French brand that are boxer shaped but brief and fairly tight-fitting. I wear what I call accident-prone clothes. If I was ever run over and taken to hospital, they'd find all my underwear colours co-ordinated with my outer wear. It's my wife's idea – she always makes sure I'm properly put together.'

The admission was not purely for comic effect. Cheryl certainly had a major role to play behind the scenes. 'I have a marvellous set-up,' he explained in an interview while appearing at Great Yarmouth's Royalty Theatre that summer – by this time, of course, he was topping the bill. 'All I have to do is concentrate on my act. Cheryl even lines up my clothes for the week ahead to cover every appointment. I might get shouted at if I pick up the wrong outfit.'

He went on: 'I was worried that friends might wonder why Cheryl had left her old life to live with a red-nosed comic. I've always thought she lowered her standards to be with me.'

But glancing around his dressing room, at the trappings of the stardom that was now his, he went on: 'This is all I'd hoped for, I love it all. Some stars complain about the pressures, the adulation, the lack of private life. That's a load of hooey. That's what I wanted all my life. I like being mobbed on the streets. I like people nudging each other saying, "Is it, yes it is, it's Michael Barrymore, *the* Michael Barrymore."'

Then there was more good news.

It was announced that Michael was to host a new show called *Strike It Lucky* for Thames TV. Admittedly, there was a little friction between the star and his producers at first. The bosses had wanted him to play it straight. 'I told them I wasn't going to stand there like a lemon, introduce contestants and get on with it,' he said. 'I insisted, "We must have fun, break a few rules." Eventually they agreed. The show is better as a result. I did a quiz show called *Get Set Go!* for the BBC recently, which didn't work, because it was too straight.'

*Strike It Lucky* was an immediate success, not least because of Michael's rapport with the audience. 'Every quiz show must dream of a Barbara Clutterbuck from Uttley,' said the *News of the World* at the time, referring to one of his contestants. 'Host Michael Barrymore struck gold with her on the first *Strike It Lucky*, his manic, messy new quiz show. "Sport," announced Barrymore, homing in on a question category. "Oooh no," she answered. "I'm not 'avin' SPORT." But sport is what we had. And so did she.'

By this time, of course, the really big money was beginning to come in. Michael and Cheryl swapped their flat for a house in Harlow that, in 1986, was worth £300,000. Soon would come the mansion in Roydon. And while Michael didn't buy a Roller, he did treat himself to a gold Mercedes. But then, he could afford to – his income was now an estimated £500,000 a year. It was a far cry from the days when the couple lived in a council flat, dined off an ironing board and lived under a bathroom ceiling that ended up in the bath. Unfortunately, Cheryl had been in the bath at the time.

# 7

# 'WE'LL LOOK STUPID IF WE TOPPLE IN THE POOL ONE NIGHT. WE CAN'T SWIM'

AS MICHAEL enjoyed the fruits of his success, Cheryl was happy to talk about a personal and professional partnership that, she insisted, suited them both down to the ground. 'Yes I wear the trousers, but not in the home,' she said. 'We're in a tough business and you've got to be tough to get up there and stay there. I've moulded Michael. I'm rough on him at times – and on myself. I have to lay down the law for both our sakes, but because he's my husband it matters much more to me what happens to him. It's not all about business.'

Whatever the nature of their business and personal relationships, it seemed to work. Michael seemed the picture of happiness. In fact, he said, as they luxuriated in their Roydon

palace complete with Jacuzzi and a huge swimming pool, they
only had one small niggle.

'The only thing that bothers me is that neither of us can
swim,' he confessed, with a smile. 'We're going to look really
stupid if we topple in one night and there isn't a soul around to
save us.' More than a decade later those words would come
back to haunt him when Stuart Lubbock lost his life in that
same pool.

At the time, though, everything looked rosy for the
twosome, even though Cheryl's early car accident had left her
with a cruel legacy. The injuries she sustained meant that she
would never be able to have children. Still, by 1986 the
Barrymores were Britain's most successful TV couple. 'If we
separated or divorced I'd still go on being his manager,' Cheryl
asserted. 'That's in our contract. I'd still be at the side of the
stage every night. We're bound together emotionally and for
business. We calmly and logically discussed what would
happen if we fell out of love, in fact we first discussed it before
we got married. We agreed that if our marriage failed we
wouldn't let it interfere with our business relationship.'

Reading between the lines, did this talk of what would
happen in the event of a split, more than ten years into the
Barrymores' apparently idyllic marriage, hint at things to
come? Cheryl, of course, knew by now that Michael had
serious problems with drink and possibly, though she couldn't

be sure, drugs. He was staying out a lot and failing to come home at night. She had not yet fully confronted the possibility that he might be having gay liaisons – that would come later. As would the public's realisation that Michael was destroying himself. For now, Michael and Cheryl appeared to be the showbiz partnership with everything.

'We are a company called Barryclair,' Cheryl continued smoothly in the interview. 'We have equal shares under the names of Michael Barrymore and Cheryl St Clair, my former stage name.'

The only problem in their marriage that the couple admitted to publicly was Cheryl's inability to become pregnant. And, during the early years of their marriage, when they were broke, they were refused permission to adopt.

'I tried very hard to have a baby, but I can't,' Cheryl sighed. 'I had operation after operation over five years. Finally, Michael said he didn't want me to have any more surgery.'

Speaking in 1986, when Michael was thirty-four, she added: 'I don't worry about hitting forty and him leaving me for a younger woman to have babies.' Ironically, of course, Michael would leave her... but only to live with other men. And even then he still wanted to adopt.

'Now we treat Michael's cabaret act as our baby – our pride and joy,' Cheryl beamed. 'We wrote it, we honed it, it's one hour and fifteen minutes of our creation and it's our greatest pleasure. We often talk business in bed, sometimes until four in the morning.

'Michael even does his act in his sleep. I hear him going through routines and taking applause. He keeps a pen and paper by his bed in case he wakes up in the night with an idea. Then he wakes me to tell me about it. If it's a joke I try to laugh, but it has to be good at 5 a.m.!

'Michael often changes the act, and if it changes for the better we keep it in. If I don't think it is, I tell him.'

Clearly, Michael and Cheryl were a dedicated team when it came to his career. And Cheryl was never backward when it came to standing up for Michael's interests – and, by implication, hers. When Michael first starred in his 'hotspot' quiz show *Strike It Lucky*, Cheryl protected every aspect of the show so fiercely that she earned the nickname 'Chainsaw Cheryl' from the production crew. Michael admitted: 'I've seen her take somebody's head off with a few lethal words. When she blows she truly blows. And she's almost always right.'

Cheryl agreed: 'I am more fiery as a manager than as a wife. I won't let people take liberties with him. In fact, I can't stand anyone taking advantage of either of us. I feel very passionate about talent. When I first saw Michael I knew he could go all the way but he needed the right person alongside him. I felt I could be that person. I'd have begged, borrowed and stolen if necessary and fought everyone. I had to fight quite a few. But I stuck to our guns and, yes, at times I didn't give a damn. We were going to have our own way.'

That said, her tough attitude had clearly paid dividends – Michael's runaway success was dramatic proof of that. 'If I hadn't taken that kind of trouble we wouldn't be where we are today,' Cheryl maintained. 'Michael wouldn't speak out. It wasn't in his nature. Now people say, "Love him – hate her." But they know they can't mess us around. This isn't just about fun. It's a business and it's fierce.

'Because I'm a woman in a man's game they probably thought we'd be easier meat, that we'd always do as we were told,' she explained, a flicker of pride in her voice. 'They soon learn otherwise... The way I look at it is it's us against the world. We have a pretty tight circle drawn around us and nobody gets in.

Fighting words. But how long would that circle remain unbroken?

**8**

# 'I WAS HER CHILD... SHE TOLD ME WHAT TO WEAR EVERY DAY'

BEHIND CLOSED doors, demons were beginning to eat away at Michael Barrymore. He'd talked light-heartedly about how Cheryl would sort out what he wore, but in truth it annoyed him more than almost anything else she did.

'I was her husband, her child, her career and her lover,' he now asserts. 'I handed over all control of my life and that's when I started to lose my way, my identity. My clothes would be laid out, there'd be Monday, Tuesday, Wednesday, Thursday, Friday outfits for work and for casual wear. One Thursday morning I picked up an outfit off the rail and Cheryl said, "What have you got on?" I said, "I'm just putting on some jeans. She said, "No, no, no, you've put the wrong one on, that's Tuesday's, this is Thursday's, that's next

Tuesday's." I took it all off and put the Thursday outfit on.

'When I started to do well and get money, I bought a car, an Audi A3, good for running around in town. She said, "Why've you got that?" I said, "I just fancy a little run-around", and she said, "Well, why have you bought that when you can afford the best?" I liked it, but it was easier to get rid of it and comply than have the hassle. I was a victim but I was the one to blame for becoming a victim.'

He confided his feelings to only a few close friends, who remained silent for years. It is only now that they feel they can speak out. One said: 'You only needed to talk to Michael for a few minutes over a drink to discover how he really felt. He believed that Cheryl had an absolutely iron grip on the marriage and she was suffocating him. He told me, "She loves order, and if I get out of order she hates it. She bloody well controls me. I was a goner from the moment I proposed."

'To be honest, if anyone needed controlling it's Michael, but it really was getting him down. I remember we were having a drink on a Tuesday and I asked him, "Is that your Tuesday suit? Did Cheryl pick that out for you?" "Yes," he said. "I'd have felt happier in a T-shirt but it isn't worth the f***ing earache."'

Michael found his solace in alcohol. He had started to drink seriously in the 1970s, when he was getting comedy gigs in London's gay clubs. Whenever he was offered a contract he would bluster and insist that he was happy to work for anyone who'd pay him, and that the kind of venue didn't matter. But he was fascinated by these places, haunts that he had long told himself were forbidden. Now he had what he considered to be a legitimate excuse to enter… and to be outrageously camp, because that was professionally the right approach to this gig. But he knew the truth. It confused and frightened him. And to quell that fear, he would drink. Eventually the drink would not be enough. There would be drugs too.

Michael loved it when drag queens and male strippers called him Michelle, when he appeared in monthly revues with the Pure Corn company. Showbiz writer Patrick Newley recalled: 'It was the booziest show in town and Barrymore was always p****d. Michael adored the whole gay scene and loved to camp about. I remember seeing him openly smacking the queens on the bottom, he also pinched them and tweaked their nipples. There was great camaraderie among the cast and there was a lot of kissing and cuddling going on. Michael used to wear make-up, wigs and women's clothes during the bawdy sketches. Besides "Michelle" they'd also call him "she" and "Miss Barrymore".' The Pure Corn Company appeared at the Theatre Royal in Stratford, east London, where most of the audience were gay men and drinking was allowed in the stalls.

Newley also revealed how Michael regularly drank a bottle

of whisky after a show and how a dressing room he shared with six transvestites and a transsexual 'with real breasts' was stacked high with cans and bottles of booze. He told the *Mirror*: 'They'd all be stripping off in front of him. Barrymore knew they were all gay but he seemed perfectly at ease with them. It was a gay show for a gay audience, littered with four-letter words and gay lingo.' But Cheryl was never seen at the shows. 'The drag queens wouldn't have liked real women hanging around,' Newley added.

Later, Michael's mother Margaret would blame the drag scene for turning her son to booze. 'He never hit the drink before, when he was working in summer shows and in respectable hotels with nice people. He was young and vulnerable and he couldn't handle things. It was all those late nights with a boozy audience.'

One comic who used to perform with Michael while he was working the club circuit told how the star would always hit the bottle after a show. Mike Jerome, a member of the New Crazy Gang comedy team, said he once saw Michael drink half a bottle of whisky, virtually straight off. 'Like a lot of people in show business, he used it to relax when he came off stage at the end of a night,' he said. 'Besides whisky he'd drink brandy or wine, depending on the mood he was in.

'The pressure of doing two or three shows in one night would really get to him. In a way he was a victim of his own

success. He had a reputation to keep up and I suppose
drinking helped him cope with it.'

It was a long time before Michael admitted to being an
alcoholic and a drug addict. A friend, who watched helplessly
as Michael spurned all efforts to get him to stop, revealed:
'He'd start on wine and move on to Jack Daniel's, usually with
Sprite, which makes it hit the bloodstream faster. Because he
was always so off the wall, it was sometimes difficult to tell
whether he was still playing to the crowd in a nightclub or was
totally off his face with booze. It was also difficult to work out
just how much he was drinking, but I reckon a bottle of Jack
Daniel's a day wouldn't be too far off the mark, maybe more
on a bad day. And God knows how much wine on top of that,
usually Chablis.

'Then came the drugs. I know that when he eventually made
a public admission of his addiction he talked about taking
speed, cocaine and ecstasy, but what that admission didn't take
account of was what he looked like to people around him. His
eyes were completely gone, red-rimmed and vacant. He could
slump so hard into a chair that it would crack and break – and
he isn't a heavy man. He also had no sense of time, he could
demand a cooked dinner at breakfast time, or breakfast at 7
p.m. There'd be stains down his shirt where wine had spilled.
When he was coherent, he'd say he was high because that's the
only way he could cope when he wasn't getting the drug he

really craved… the applause of an audience. It was as if he was taken over by some form of inner beast that told him, "If you can't have them, let me have you instead."

'A lot of us tried to get him to stop, but you couldn't watch him twenty-four hours a day and there were always people who'd be keen to buy him a drink, much like George Best. They must have seen what it was doing to him, but still they'd press another glass in his hand. Michael was happy, he had an audience, it was all he'd ever wanted.'

9

# 'I'D START DRINKING THEN MOVE ON TO PILLS'

DESPITE THE drinking and the drug taking, despite seething inside at what he believed was his wife's iron control, despite the split with his family and despite the non-stop working, Michael Barrymore just about managed to hold everything together. Until July 1988.

It should have been a great summer. He was hosting a BBC series called *Michael Barrymore's Saturday Night Out*, a variety show filmed in Jersey, and was already a star with *Strike It Lucky*.

The *Saturday Night Out* show was everything the public had come to expect: barely controlled lunacy finished off with a spoof of *Come Dancing* featuring June Brown, who plays Dot Cotton in *EastEnders*. 'You carry on,' she told him, amazed at his manic energy. 'I'm going to have a fag.'

He continued to play summer season, still throwing out the odd member of the audience, and finally revealing where that particular part of the act originated. A huge biker had been to see him when he was compering at Croydon's Fairfield Hall. 'He was your typical biker,' Michael explained, 'and he carried his goggles and huge leather gauntlets under his arm. On the spur of the moment, I jumped down from the stage and said, "Yes?" The poor guy looked baffled. I told him the Masonic Hall was next door and that he was at a private party. "No, it's not a gag. Off you go! Clear off! This is totally private." And he went!

'I never thought I'd get away with it again, but it's proved a real winner. I make the public part of the act and they enjoy it. Suddenly they can tell their pals, "I was thrown out by Michael Barrymore." They never forget it.'

But in July his drinking grew out of control. Finally, something snapped and he collapsed, apparently from exhaustion. Doctors ordered him to stop working seven nights a week. At the time, Cheryl told the press, 'Michael was doing too much by working every possible moment. His routine really takes it out of him and he loses at least 4 pounds [in weight] every night. Michael is getting older and can't keep up the pace.' But he was only thirty-six!

Looking back on those days now, Michael spells out exactly what his excesses involved. 'By then I was drinking on a constant basis, every day, then taking prescribed tablets as well just to get the feeling of something removing me from where I was. I didn't want to experience any time that I wasn't working. I'd immediately start drinking and taking pills or whatever... just to get me totally away.' Reflecting on why he lost control so dramatically, he also saw his behaviour as something of a rebellion: 'I was rebelling against all the things I'd been modelled on, the gratitude, the staying quiet off stage. I didn't want to be that nice person any more, I wanted to experience some sort of notoriety.

'I couldn't live my life on stage twenty-four hours a day. But when I came off I couldn't replace that feeling. I had no identity of my own outside of my work, so that's why I tried to work non-stop. On stage is the only place I feel content and happy, the one place I don't need to feed my disease with drink or drugs. Take me out of that and I'm not sure I have a clue who I am.'

In August 1988, with the problems in his personal life growing by the day, he played a live show at the Bournemouth International Centre. And still the audience lapped it up. 'That's the band and believe me, they should be!' he laughed. 'Don't roll your eyes at me, luv, 'cos I'll just pick 'em up and roll them back!' There were impersonations of Alan Whicker, Boy George and Danny la Rue. Then a member of the audience – an elderly member – was dragged up on stage for the *Swan Lake* routine. Michael was as fond of dancing with women of a certain age as he had been in his Redcoat days.

But after the show Michael appeared drunk and dishevelled in his hotel, the four-star Palace Court. He had gone for a night out with his co-star, comedian Hal Nolan. When Michael returned he grabbed the hotel assistant manager, James Lloyd, in an extremely delicate place. Australian Mitchell Gorrick, who worked at the hotel as night porter, revealed: 'It was totally bizarre. First I heard a crashing noise on the stairs. I saw Barrymore stumbling down with Nolan shouting, "No Michael!"'

'Barrymore seemed drunk. They both went out and returned about 2 a.m. Nolan helped him upstairs and on the way chatted to me. He said, "I've known Michael for about three years and he takes a bit of looking after."'

'Later, Barrymore lurched back down to the lobby with his shirt hanging out. I asked him if there was anything we could do to help, but he just slumped into a leather couch. He was smoking a cigarette and letting the ash fall all over him. He wasn't aware of where he was or why he was there.

'The other night porter went off duty and I asked James Lloyd, the assistant manager, to stay on to help. At around 5.30 a.m. Barrymore got up, walked over to the porter's desk where we were standing and grabbed at James's crotch. James told him unceremoniously to "F\*\*\* off!"'

The incident made the papers but loyal Cheryl, determined to exercise some damage control, issued a statement that, though it was clearly intended to provide reassurance at the time, was to prove ironic given the subsequent course of relationship: 'Mr Barrymore is a normal heterosexual male. I have been married to him for thirteen years.'

A friend of Michael's who knew him well during that summer season of shows, revealed: 'Cheryl was doing her best, but the tide of Michael's inner torment was too much to turn back. Eventually he had a complete breakdown and he was taken away to a rehab clinic. I think the official explanation was that he had been working too hard and needed a rest. But in truth they were trying to wean him off drink and drugs. God knows what would have happened if they hadn't. He could have ended up dead somewhere.'

When Michael emerged from rehab, his career was still on track, though the gossip about his off-stage life was now spreading like wildfire. Still, his live and TV performances would always see him 'Awight', a word that had already become one of the most famous catchphrases in Britain.

In December 1989, Michael was everywhere. He hosted a Christmas Day edition of *Strike It Lucky* and appeared in pantomime as Wishee Washee in Aladdin at London's Dominion Theatre – his first West End lead role. Boxing hero Frank Bruno was his co-star and Michael clearly enjoyed the challenge of this new form of entertainment. 'Frank is full of it, know what I mean?' he grinned, in an interview he gave during the pantomime run. 'We set each other off and once he starts he never stops. He's at his best when he makes things up as he goes along. I guess we'll have to stick to the script to some degree, though.'

The pantomime was another step forward for a different reason: it was Michael's West End debut and he relished every moment of it. 'It's the first time I've done a season in a London theatre,' he revealed. 'It's something very special to me. I've been trying to find out why it's taken me twenty odd years to make it across the Thames from south London where I was born to the West End via every other town and city in England. After all, it's only a few stops on the Tube.'

It appeared that Michael was also starting to relax more. He had even started talking about taking a holiday. 'I'll try to get away after the pantomime but if I don't book it now, something is bound to come along and make it impossible,' he said. 'The thing is with performers that after years of nothing – no money, no offers and looking at four brick walls with no phone ringing – when the work comes, it all comes at once.'

Michael and Cheryl took off to Florida for a month for a much-needed rest, not least because Michael's weight had plummeted to 10 stone through the sheer grind of hard work. 'I hadn't had a day off in a year and I suppose my body's simply had enough,' he explained when he returned. 'I'm always slim, but I'd lost about a stone and a half. In this business you can work night and day without ever realising the damage it's doing to you. It was the first real holiday I've had in years and I feel better for it. A friend lent us his mansion in Palm Beach, right next to places owned by the Kennedys and the Trumps. It was fabulous and we just rested by the pool in the sun.'

But Michael was not going to stay away from work for long. As well as another series of *Strike It Lucky*, he had signed up for a new game show called *Plaza*, to be set in a department store, although in fact it was never to materialise. Yet he was still the undisputed king of prime-time TV.

If ever proof were needed of that, it came in 1990, when the last three episodes of Chris Tarrant's quiz show *Everybody's Equal* were dropped to make room for more episodes of *Strike It Lucky*. Tarrant was pulling in a very respectable 8 million viewers, but even that couldn't compete with Michael's fan base. He was now averaging 14 million viewers a show. There was talk of a series in the US and a sitcom. And, of course, the live act was still stunning – especially his routine at that year's Night of a Hundred Stars at the London Palladium.

Amazingly, he'd also found a hobby! He had started a collection of wind-up toys after doctors told him to slow down. The collection was now fully catalogued and worth a fortune. 'They told me I was overworking,' he smiled. 'So I found a hobby where wind-up motors do the work.' Then, in his very next sentence, Michael revealed something of the major effect that his early family life had had on him: 'In a way, these toys are making up for my childhood. That was the worst time of my life.'

Michael held one of his toys in his hand, looked at it thoughtfully and added: 'My dad disappeared like someone in an Agatha Christie novel. Just upped and went. I don't know if he's still alive. It's doubtful, because I'm sure he'd have contacted me. Over the years I've often wondered if he'd suddenly turn up as I got more well known – the way John Lennon's father did. I've been on television so much during the last year that he must have seen me. Barrymore isn't my real name, but I don't suppose my face has changed all that much since I was eleven.'

But though his professional life was going from strength to strength, there were worries on Michael's personal front. Cheryl's father Eddie, the man who had helped the couple so much, died of cancer. And around the same time, Michael's brother John Parker gave a newspaper interview in which he accused Michael of disowning his family following his rise to fame. The interview dripped with John's bitterness over their bust-up and the failure of the shop.

John, who said Michael hadn't spoken to him for eight

years, hit out: 'The public see this Mr Nice Guy but they don't know he won't even speak to his own flesh and blood. He says that he was beaten by his dad but that's rubbish. Dad never laid a finger on Michael because I wouldn't let him. And he never protected Mum, he was always cowering in his room while I dealt with it.

'Michael also suggests he had no toys as a child,' John continued. 'But what he doesn't tell people is that I used to bring him Matchbox cars every Friday night. I'd just started my first job and used to pay one shilling and sixpence (7 1/2p) for the cars and Michael loved them. It was a lot for me at the time, because I wasn't earning much. But now he's rich and famous, he doesn't remember.'

And recalling the last time they met, at a Wimpy around the corner from Michael's mother's home in 1982, John went on: 'I asked if he was going round to see Mum. He answered, "For Christ's sake don't tell Mum I'm here. I haven't got time to go and see her." But that's Michael's problem: now that he's made it, he hasn't got time for Mum or any of us. He bought me a burger and chips. The bill came to 85p and he paid. That's all he's ever given me in his life. And I haven't set eyes on him since.'

Michael's sister Anne was far more reluctant to talk, but added in the same interview: 'If only Michael knew what he was doing to Mum by freezing the family out like this. It's destroying her. Mum does tell me that Michael slips her money now and again and has even phoned occasionally, but he doesn't tell Cheryl. I think he's scared that if she found out she'd hit the roof. Mum phoned me a few days ago and was sobbing her heart out on the phone. She's normally a strong woman, but she keeps saying she wants Michael back in the family again before she dies. She used to be so full of spirit, but now she's depressed and weary.' Still, Anne added: 'I love his shows and aside from all the bitterness, I'm proud of what he's done. I wish we could just let the past be the past and make up.'

At least Michael's bank manager was happy – his client was richer than ever. Michael kept announcing that each new series of *Strike It Lucky* would be his last, but each time he was persuaded back in to the studio to record more of the programmes. By 1991 he was earning £100,000 for making just the that show, on top of which he landed a three-year £500,000 deal with London Weekend Television. The critics continued to rave, not least because of Michael's skill with an audience. More than anyone, he could make stars of so-called ordinary people.

'I've always suspected it and now I know for sure,' one reviewer began. 'If you want to become a loudmouth with as much front as Woolworths, change your name to Roseanne. There she was last night on *Strike It Lucky*, our very own raucous Roseanne from Edinburgh. The lass with the Andy Stewart legs and the tartan accent made Roseanne Barr look positively classy. "I'm great at bumping my gums,' she shrieked. 'And before you ask, that's Scottish for rabbiting." And on and on she went. It was no wonder she and boyfriend Mark won the show outright – he obviously spends his life with his nose buried in an encyclopaedia just to escape her.'

Also in 1991, Michael was signed up for a series on London Weekend Television called *Barrymore At Large*, later titled simply *Barrymore*, in which he was to pop up unexpectedly in unlikely places all over the country. 'Michael's great strength is in chatting up the public,' said a source at LWT. 'We've dreamed up some crazy places for him to appear.'

That summer he was starring at the Princess Theatre Torquay and getting rave reviews. 'Calling Michael Barrymore's act "stand-up comedy" is like calling an Uzi 9mm a handgun,' said one newspaper. 'He hardly stands at all – not still, anyway.'

According to the glowing review, Michael was careering about like a human squash ball on plastic legs. He was up to all the old favourites: three girls arrived late and Michael pounced. 'Yes? Can we help?' he asked, inspecting the tickets. One, inevitably, was deemed to be for another night and the hapless girl found herself banished from the theatre – followed shortly afterwards by a man who laughed at Michael's singing.

He then excelled himself by throwing out a whole row of people before dancing with a middle-aged lady called Pam and branding another member of the audience a Lybian spy. Once again, his act left the theatre begging for more.

Ever the perfectionist, though, Michael now began worrying that his television shows were not up to his stage performances, something he hoped *Barrymore At Large* would put right. 'I don't seem to be able to capture the lunacy from my stage shows,' he complained. 'They are like manic one-man Monty Python shows. This is the first time that I've felt we've captured the real thing. I consider myself the co-star with the audience as the stars. I get them on stage to show us their party pieces of a karaoke spot and they're hilarious.' Asked how it differed from *That's Life*, Esther Rantzen's long-running show, Michael quipped, 'I'm not a woman and I haven't got buck teeth.'

Of course, success did come at a price. Michael might have loved being mobbed in the street, but he wasn't so happy with the rumours circulating about his health. He was as thin as ever, and some people were now whispering that he was seriously ill. 'I've got a clean bill of health and I haven't got any illnesses,' snapped Michael in a newspaper interview. 'I saw doctors last week for insurance purposes and I'm fine. I don't know why people keep saying I'm ill.'

Cheryl was equally irritated by all the attention her

husband's health was attracting. 'People are saying Michael's ill when he's not, he's right as rain,' she complained. 'But are they trying to imply something more?'

Michael reacted in his own inimitable fashion: while appearing at the British Comedy Awards he announced: 'I'm getting an award. Slimmer of the Year.' It was a joke to cover a serious problem. Michael's weight had fallen again, once more from 12 to 10 stone – dangerously thin for a 6-foot-3-inch man. By now, the gay rumours surrounding him were also gaining in strength, at a time when worries over Aids were rife. In November of that year, gay Queen star Freddie Mercury died after contracting the disease. Attention focused on Michael's frame, which now looked decidedly wasted.

Michael and Cheryl decided to take a break at Florida's Key West, not realising that it was a famously gay resort. When Michael was told, he insisted he was only going for the deep sea fishing and wasn't going to cancel. Anyway, he and Cheryl had already booked a £500-a-night beachside apartment at the luxurious Casa Marina resort.

A picture taken during their holiday, showing Michael sunbathing on the sands, was shattering to behold. He looked gaunt and ill and his ribs were sticking out. It was published under the headline 'The Real Thin' a pun on Coca-Cola's slogan 'It's the real thing' and was accompanied by a picture of a Coke bottle with Michael's head superimposed on it.

Reading between the lines, and taking into account the play on the word 'coke', it seemed the paper were implying something else about Michael's lifestyle too...

Michael tried to blame his bad physical shape on work pressures. 'I was knackered, that's all,' he insisted at the time. 'There's nothing wrong – I just get worn out and forget to eat.' And Cheryl stressed: 'Michael isn't ill. He looks thin because he is thin.'

For the moment, most people seemed to accept these reassurances at face value. Michael flew back from his American holiday in January 1992 and said he was 'completely fit and raring to go'. After arriving at Heathrow, he made light of the stories that had circulated in his absence and said: 'I had a very relaxing holiday and put on some weight. I ate a lot of ice cream and I'm now pleased to have a tummy.'

In April 1992, Michael won the ITV Personality of the Year award from the Television and Radio Industries Club. Better still, his new series, *Barrymore*, was starting. And as ever, 'normal' people were the stars. This. more than any other show was Michael returning to his comic roots, clowning around and simply interacting with members of the public. 'We had some real characters turning up when we were filming,' said Michael. 'I do seem to have a knack of making people relax. They know they're going to be safe with me. They'll be slightly sent up, of course. But I never ridicule them. The art of it is asking them to do something, then letting them run with it. If, when I'm interviewing people, I get a reaction from the audience, I'll let them get on with it. It's my job to set it up in the first place and if it's not going well, then I join in and muck about.'

Other stars were happy to let Michael take the mick out of them, too. During a live performance at the Circus Tavern nightclub in Purfleet, Essex, in March 1992, Michael spotted a famous face in the audience. 'Oi, Libyan! Get out!' he shouted, before leaping from the stage and marching boxer Nigel Benn to the door. A broadly grinning Benn tried to return to his seat several times before he was finally allowed to stay… then Michael spent the rest of the evening making jokes at his expense. 'I didn't mind being made a fool of,' said Nigel afterwards. 'I think Michael's terrific and I was more than happy to go along with the joke.'

In 1992 Michael also won the ITV Personality of the Year award and spent the summer season at the Futurist Theatre in Scarborough – although, in a nod to his superstar status he was now performing only two nights a week.

And, proving that he had lost none of the lightning wit that had made him a star in the first place, he recovered from a moment that would have floored many a lesser performer. 'Where's your daddy?' he asked seven-year-old Holly Johnson who had come from Wakefield in Yorkshire to watch the show. 'I don't have a daddy,' she replied. 'Aaaah,' went the audience, as one, and wondered how Michael would get out of that one. 'Never mind,' he replied, putting his arm around her. 'I didn't have a daddy when I was your age. It's not necessarily a bad thing. There's more room around the house.'

But off stage Michael was only just coming to terms with the loss of his own father-figure, Eddie Cocklin. He had used his death as another reason to turn to drink. 'It's only after the event that I can analyse just what went wrong,' he said later in an interview, with reference to his drinking. 'And one of the major factors was losing Cheryl's dad. When he died, it left a void in our lives. It's difficult to explain, but Eddie was a real father to me – a dad I'd never had. It was a huge emotional loss. He was a man in a million – a friend and a guide, personally and professionally. No one had ever cared for me and my interests the way Eddie did. So on a practical level, it was equally tough. Cheryl's my manager, but Eddie looked after the business side of things – he did it all. Then suddenly he was gone. I'd never lost anyone I was close to before. I realised with Eddie's loss that the day a parent or mentor dies is the day you grow up and stop being a child. You're alone and it's very frightening.

'What I suffered was the most tremendous delay of grief. I understand now that everyone must grieve, but I couldn't do it like other people. I saw Cheryl and her mum cry and I couldn't. I was unable to express my terrible feeling of isolation. Eddie had been a great influence. He was very strict and only let us take wages out of our earnings. He never let us buy anything we couldn't afford. Eddie harnessed me really, because before that my attitude had been, "Easy come, easy go." The truth is that two years on, I still miss him. Especially now that *Barrymore*, which he helped us to achieve, is such a success. He would have loved that.'

# 10

# 'I WAS HIDING MY BOOZE IN CANS OF COKE'

CHRISTMAS ARRIVED and with it came panto. This year it was Aladdin at Manchester's Opera House for Michael. The greasepaint covered his anguish at the problems that were mounting in his personal life; by his own admission, Michael Barrymore was good at covering up the truth. 'I was hiding my drink at dinner,' he now says, with searing honesty. 'Putting half of it in a can of Coke as if I was just drinking Coke... doing anything just to get the stuff, as much as I thought I needed, which would be far excess of what anybody would need. And the thought was, "If it runs out, what am I going to do?" And I'd run out and end up in a club or wherever, end up back at whoever's flat. I thought what was really wrong with me was that I was gay. That's what I thought was the route of the whole problem. But I couldn't say even in a private room what the problem was. I would say it was everything else, whatever the doctors and psychiatrists would come up with I'd say, "Yeah, that, that's how I feel." I thought if I told the truth I'd lose my career, which was my identity.

'More and more I was using drink to make me brave enough to go out,' he admitted. 'Sometimes I'd deliberately start a row with Cheryl just so I'd be able to say, "Look what you've done, you've made me go out", as an excuse. Then I'd wander out and go to clubs and end up at some strangers' houses. Finally I'd wake up and think, where am I?, then try to find my way back home. Cheryl would be waiting for me and I'd just break down and cry. But if I indulged myself in drink and drugs, that would make me feel I wouldn't have to deal with it.'

And for the time being, his lies were keeping his career on track. It seemed that everything Michael touched was turning to gold – Aladdin took £1.4 million, making it, at that time, the highest grossing pantomime in history. The run was extended by two weeks and a total of 150,000 people saw the show. In February 1993 Michael won a Variety Club award for ITV Personality of the Year. 'At last, the man from Del Fonte, he say yes,' he joked, holding up his award to Lord Delfont, Variety Club chairman.

But in the same month, some of the gloss was taken off his success when police were called to Manchester's Britannia

Hotel after a 4 a.m. bust-up. Michael had gone straight to the hotel bar from the Opera House. After a bout of drinking he homed in on hotel guest Chris Shelley

'I didn't recognise who it was at first,' said Chris. 'Then he came over to our table. You could tell he was very drunk. He tried to introduce himself, but we couldn't make out what he was saying. He was staring in to space like a zombie. I don't know whether it was the drink, but I didn't say anything because of who he is. He was at our table for half an hour. At one stage someone said something and he said, "F*** that", but he didn't swear again.

'Then he leaned over and asked me to come with him for a quiet word. We went out of the bar and he told me two guys were after him. He said he wanted somewhere to hide and asked what room I was in, but I wouldn't tell him. I said I was willing to help but needed to know more. You don't hand out your room number because someone says they want to hide. It all struck me as strange. As we were talking, someone else came through the doors and Michael ran off.'

Michael, who wasn't even a guest at the four-star hotel, was later heard banging on a hotel room door, yelling 'Open up!' The police were called but by the time they arrived Michael was walking down the stairs. Laughing off the incident, he later said: 'I'm awight now but sometimes I'm not sure I'm on the same planet.'

After another Florida holiday with Cheryl, it was back to work. There was continued talk about Michael starring in a sitcom, and there was another summer season to look forward to, this time at the Bournemouth International Centre. True to form, Michael was up to his old tricks: branding members of the audience Libyan terrorists, chucking out guests, inviting elderly ladies up on stage to do the lambada and generally causing mayhem.

The audience lapped it up. 'I'd rather cycle through Bosnia in a target T-shirt than sit in the front row of a Barrymore show,' said one reviewer before concluding: '6ft 3in Michael is a giant of an entertainer. He's Barry brilliant.'

Michael was still exhausted though, and was forced to cancel four performances of the show to seek help for stress at the Marchwood Priory again. The official reason for the cancellation had been a 'sore throat', but the Priory is one of the country's top private clinics for sufferers of acute stress and problems related to alcohol, drugs and eating. During three days of treatment Michael underwent group therapy sessions and coaching in relaxation methods such as yoga.

He later admitted that he'd had a breakdown due to his workload. Michael had recorded twenty-eight episodes of *Strike It Lucky* in fifteen days, then moved on to the summer season at Bournemouth, fitting in rehearsals for his *Barrymore* TV show.

'But no amount of therapy was going to get to the heart of his problem,' said a pal, 'because, as he now admits himself, he never confessed he was gay – and keeping the secret was what was tearing him up inside. He'd sit in some white room, or lie on a couch and talk about his upbringing till the cows came home But he was a performer, for God's sake, he spent his life giving his audiences what they wanted to hear and now he was giving psychiatrists what he thought they wanted to hear. So no one was really getting to the root of his problem.' He wanted his fans to laugh with him, not at him. And his career was the most precious thing he had, more precious than his marriage, certainly. If he and Cheryl were still sleeping together by this time, it must have been very infrequently.

When Michael emerged from the clinic he returned to Bournemouth's Pavilion Theatre after cancelling shows over the weekend. He even laughed and joked about his treatment. 'It did me good being in that place,' he told the audience. 'You don't have to be insane to go there. I'm not completely mad. They say I'm mad, but I'm not really mad.'

He received a standing ovation. It felt good to be home.

Speaking later about his condition before he entered the Priory, he admitted: 'I've never felt so awful. I knew I needed help.' Cheryl choked back tears and said: 'I was shocked at how bad he was. He's my world, he's all I've got. I don't want to lose him – I'll have nothing. I hadn't seen Michael like that since my father Eddie died. Eddie was the father Michael never had and Michael adored him.

'His doctor has told him he's got to have more rest and continue his treatment. It will be an ongoing process and Michael will be going back to the clinic.'

A couple of months later, in October, there were yet more concerns about his health, but they only served to prompt an outpouring of affection from his adoring public, with a flood of faxes pouring in to newspaper offices in support. 'You'll be awight Mike. Thanks for all the laughs you give us on TV,' said Ken and Cath Taylor from Halifax, West Yorkshire, in a note to the *News of the World*. 'You're a lovely, caring person,' said Irene Hunter, from Gosport, Hampshire. 'You made my night when you took me up on stage in Bournemouth and sang "Crazy" to me. Please keep on smiling.' Sharon Livingstone of Birmingham even composed a poem for the troubled entertainer:

> *Some folk get stressed and eat willy nilly,*
> *They end up quite fat and look very silly.*
> *Some people just fret and get very thin,*
> *It affects us all, you just can't win.*
> *So come on, our Michael, and eat like a pig,*
> *We all want you well to do that next gig.*

But Michael decided there were to be fewer 'next gigs'. Guided by Cheryl, he cut his workload by about 50 per cent. She even tore up her workaholic husband's first movie deal. It was to have been a straight part in a multi-million pound comedy, something they'd spent years longing for. Cheryl also cancelled two lucrative foreign tours for 1994, to New Zealand and Australia, and shelved plans to make a *Barrymore* series Down Under.

In an interview at the time, Cheryl hugged Michael and said: 'No money is worth this worry and stress – and he had to be told the work was taking its toll again. Now it's clear this is obviously something that's recurring, I've put my foot down. I thought it would never happen again and this time I'm very worried.'

Yet again Michael vowed he was going to quit *Strike It Lucky*, as well as cancelling a pre-Christmas stage show in London and a season scheduled for the following summer in Blackpool (later reinstated on a shorter run). He was determined, however, to go ahead with 1993's Royal Variety Performance in front of the Queen. But he announced it was his last live performance and no one could fail to feel the wave of affection for him that welled up from the audience.

Of course, the show was a resounding success. The audience howled with laughter as Michael messed around with the 1st Battalion of the Kings Regiment. 'I love you,' he whispered to the sergeant major, bringing the house down. And it wasn't just the audience in the theatre that lapped it up. So did the fans at home, with ratings rocketing from the average 14 million for a Royal Variety Performance to 17 million.

'I'm gobsmacked after Saturday night,' said an elated Michael. 'The telegrams I've received since the show probably explain how I feel.' And with that, he went on to read a series of spoof telegrams from, amongst others, Prince Harry and John Major.

*Strike It Lucky* and *Barrymore* were both pulling in 14 million viewers and he was nominated in 1993's British Comedy Awards for three prizes: Top Variety Performer, Best Entertainment Series and Top ITV Presenter, the last two of which he won. (Ken Dodd got the Variety prize.) 'There's no funnier comic in Britain today than Michael Barrymore,' declared critic Michael Hellicar. 'He charges round the TV studios like a pipe cleaner on speed,' said Pauline Wallin in the newspaper *Today*. Michael was becoming more than just a popular entertainer; he was fast turning in to a national institution. 'I know I'm lucky to have got where I am,' he said. 'It's like winning the jackpot. So life's a bit of awight. Wight?'

Guest of honour at the Awards night was his psychiatrist Dr Austin Tate. 'It ain't cheap but my psychiatrist has completely changed my life,' Michael announced. 'I'm so much healthier than I was a few months ago. I feel great. A year ago I couldn't open up and talk to people the way I do now. Austin and I have become very good friends in addition to him being my psychiatrist. He comes with me to all the big events in my life, such as recordings and award ceremonies, to give him a better insight in to my world. It's important for him to see me when I'm under pressure so he can understand me better. But he doesn't give me advice. He just lets me talk and I make my own decisions.

'It really has made a huge difference. Just a year ago I didn't enjoy coming to events like this. Without him, going on stage at the Comedy Awards would have been a huge ordeal for me. I used to worry about how I speak – now I don't worry about that any more. I'm learning how to relax and cope with the pressure.'

Michael was also well aware of the secret that made him so popular and able to take such risks with his audience. 'It doesn't matter how talented you are,' he said. 'It doesn't matter how clever you are, what a wonderful voice you've got or how brilliantly you dance if, when people look at you, they don't like you as a person.

'It's what Tommy Cooper had. Nobody was more off-the-wall than Cooper, he was a load of rubbish, but you loved the man and you trusted him, and if he thought it was funny, you did.'

An unlikely fan of Michael's, Frank Skinner, agreed. 'I like the way you feel with Michael Barrymore,' he said. 'You feel he has a lot more brain than your average "this bloke walks in to a pub" type of comic. I feel in a way he's on the wrong circuit, that he should be working with French and Saunders, people like that.'

The thought had clearly occurred to Michael too: 'I do get on very well with the alternative crowd,' he admitted. 'I seem to have trotted along the middle. There was that little war going on for a while, wasn't there? One lot slagging off the other lot. [Ben] Elton firing off here. And then Tarbuck. I carried on through the middle. Every time I met them at do's, Stephen Fry would come up to me and say, "I really enjoy your work." And then Ben Elton would say, "I'm a real big fan." It's not the sort of programme you have to work out. If it makes you forget for an hour, it's done its job. If I wanted to do anything else, I'd go on Channel 4 and go in Rory's spot. I get on well with Rory and I get on well with what's left of the mainstream.

'The accepted wisdom from a number of critics, though, is that I've got it all wrong, that you shouldn't have kids and eighty-year olds and blokes doing farmyard impressions on telly. But the whole idea is to open the door to the sort of people who can't normally get on telly.'

Michael also had the gift of being tender on TV without slipping into schmaltz. In a special Christmas edition of *Strike*

*It Lucky*, he talked to a nurse who cradled a Warrington bomb victim in her arms, as well as a series of children who, although ill themselves, competed to raise money for charity. They included his old friend Holly.

'Michael and most of the studio audience were in tears,' said one television insider after the recording. 'It's one of the most moving programmes going out this Christmas.'

But that December was also memorable for a far stranger surprise. During a recording of his Barrymore show, hundreds saw Michael look shaken when his guest, the medium Doris Collins, passed on a message from beyond the grave – a message from his dead father-in-law, Eddie.

Doris, then seventy-five, had been invited on the show to talk about her psychic gift. But as Michael chatted to her, she said someone from the 'other side' had been with her all day wanting to pass on a message to him.

He identified himself as 'one of the firm' and said he 'wanted his dues'. Michael knew at once who Doris was talking about. As she spoke, he whispered: 'I know who it is, it's Eddie. I miss him dreadfully.'

Doris explained that Eddie's talking about 'his dues' meant he wanted Michael to balance stardom with inner happiness and enjoy his success. Michael added: 'Eddie wanted nothing more than for me to be a success. That's what he worked for. But he wouldn't have wanted me to have success and not my health.'

Michael then told the audience: 'I feel more at ease with the man or woman on the street than I could ever do with showbiz people. I get on OK with showbiz people when I work with them but I don't socialise in those circles. I'd rather go fishing with the bloke up the road then go to a showbiz party. That's why I drive myself so hard – because I don't want to let people down. If people pay their hard-earned money to go and see me I don't want to disappoint them. I always try to give 100 per cent.'

Cheryl said later: 'Michael didn't know Doris had a message for him when he started the interview. Doris told me she had a message for Michael in the afternoon and asked whether she should tell him. I knew it would be OK.'

Cheryl's mum, Eddie's widow Kitty, was sitting in the audience as the show was being recorded at ITV's studios in south-east London. After coming off stage, Michael said: 'Eddie is never far from my thoughts. Even before the Royal Variety Show I had a few doubts about whether what I was going to do was right. But then I thought of Eddie and what he'd have said – "Sod it – go for it. You're as good as anyone."'

By the following January, Michael appeared to be firing on all cylinders again. His first act of 1994 was to pose with The Chippendales – in a latex body suit. His show *Barrymore* was back on TV and the public loved it more than ever. 'Brilliant Michael Barrymore is as unpredictable as a San Fernando earth tremor – and almost as disruptive,' wrote one critic. And, as usual, children and old age pensioners kept stealing the show. Barrymore's face was a comedy act in itself as he watched ten-year old Chalkie Adams from Ramsgate in Kent mimicking Max Miller's old joke, which started with the line 'I am a little dove and I've had a little love' and ended with 'I am a little duck – and I thank you.'

Other shows had him joining a troupe of Ukrainian dancers, roller-skating and sending up James Cagney in a spoof of the musical *Yankee Doodle Dandy*. And week in, week out, increased success was bringing increased rewards. He treated himself to a £182,000 Bentley Continental that he'd fallen in love with from the moment he'd set eyes on it in a garage in London's Berkley Square. 'It's a lovely motor,' he said proudly. 'They only make around seventy and most go for export. You don't see many in Britain.' He also spent £5,000 on a ED1 number plate in honour of father-in-law Eddie.

Then came another prize: Showbiz Personality of the Year. Michael used his own acceptance speech to parody every acceptance speech ever made. 'I would like to thank Sir Peter Hall, who gave me the opportunity to try out my little play at the Aldwych back in 1958. That is how it all began… ' he started. Luckily, the luvvies loved it and Michael received a standing ovation. He followed this by signing a £250,000 deal to advertise Cadbury's chocolate fingers.

But it wasn't all sunshine and roses. Less than a month after the award, Michael's mother Margaret gave an interview to the *Sunday Mirror* in which she told how her son had cut off all contact with her in June 1990 without, she said, a word of explanation.

Margaret also insisted that, despite his public comments to the contrary, Michael's childhood had been a happy one. 'He lived with me until he was twenty-one,' she told the interviewer. 'But now I never see or hear from him. Now I'm trying to make peace.' She sighed: 'The night before he married Cheryl, he said to me: "Everything is going to change for you. You'll have everything you ever wanted. But it hasn't turned out that way."'

She went on: 'It's strange to see your son on TV and not see him in real life. I love his shows, *Strike It Lucky* and *Barrymore*. I sit there and laugh my head off. Sometimes I shed a few tears as well.'

Margaret was especially hurt by Michael's account of his anguished childhood. 'He was a lovely boy,' she said. 'He was never deprived of anything apart from the fact that he didn't have a dad from the age of nine. He used to bring his friends back here all the time for meals. He was proud of the fact that I was a good cook and he liked to show them. It's sad the way it has turned out. And I know that, as his mother, this separation from his family is not doing him any good.'

Michael's sister Anne was also quoted in the *Sunday Mirror* interview, as was his brother John, then fifty-one, who took the opportunity to lambast Cheryl in print. 'I think she wears the trousers,' he told the same newspaper. 'My mother wrote him a letter a couple of years ago and she rang my sister saying, "What's your mother doing, writing to my husband?"'

But if Michael thought the publicity would dent his popularity, he needn't have worried. That same month he was again voted ITV Personality of the Year in the Radio and Television Industry's Club awards.

He was also becoming more daring in his television shows. Well, the audience thought it was daring. Backroom staff who knew about the secret life Michael led were beginning to wonder whether his two worlds were beginning to collide, as stranger and stranger people appeared with him on screen. One was Carolyne Munroe, who had started life as a man before having a sex change operation. Another was Janett Scotta, a transvestite.

'Is this too early in the evening?' asked the critics. Michael leapt to his own defence. 'My show is an open book,' he said. 'You can't be a man of the people without inviting all sorts of people on. I believe in live and let live. I don't think you should tuck anyone away at twelve at night.'

He started taking yet more risks. 'The other day I did a routine completely off the cuff,' he said. 'Utterly unscripted.

We only had a minute to go. That's how serious it was. I came down the stairs and said, 'Michael Barrymore's not my real name. It's Judy Garland.' It was pure inspiration. I got the trombonist out of the band and started doing this Garland number, "You Made Me Love You". I thought, I don't know how I'm going to get out of this! But the band picked it up really well.'

Nothing had come of his talks with US television channels, but the British stations were keener on Michael than ever. His contract with LWT was coming up for renewal and the BBC made no secret of the fact that they would like to poach him. 'Michael is the hottest name on TV,' confirmed a BBC executive. 'Viewers love him because he's so good with people.'

He was also receiving praise from the a new generation of comedians. Joe Pasquale, who had appeared on *Barrymore* with Bradley Walsh, revealed that he had long been a fan. 'I saw Michael perform one night and after the show I went round the back to get an autograph,' he said. 'I asked him how I could become a comic and he told me to perform wherever I could and as often as possible. His closing words were, "You never know, we might end up on the same bill one day." And that's what really chuffed me most.'

Rumours were flying around the gangly celebrity with the cheeky patter: that the BBC wanted Michael to front *The*

*Generation Game*; that LWT was offering him £1.2 million to stay; that Thames was one the verge of offering him £3.5 million... Michael dealt with the stress in his usual way: in May he slipped off to Florida with Cheryl. But he didn't stay in the sunshine, instead he checked into the Ashley House Clinic near Baltimore, Ohio. He signed in under the name of Michael P, using his old initial for Parker, and spent three weeks drying out in another attempt to beat his addiction to whisky and pills.

The £3,000-a-week facility was run by reformed alcoholic priest, Father Joseph Martin. It's telling motto is Through Death To Life. Patients at Ashley House take part in group therapy and Alcoholics Anonymous meetings, and listen to 69-year-old Father Martin's lectures. A tearful Michael told fellow patients how secret binges on Scotch, bourbon and Irish whiskey had reduced him to a sozzled wreck. He also admitted to them that he had chewed chunks of marijuana and swallowed painkillers and tranquillisers.

One patient recalled his first impressions of the TV star in an interview with the *Mirror*: 'I was sitting on the steps outside having a smoke when I saw this tall, really gangly guy staggering out of a car with a friend. He was visibly shaky, unsteady and bleary eyed.' He added: 'I later learned he had flown from his home in Palm Beach and he admitted to me, "Yeah, I drank on the plane, didn't I. I had the last drink as the wheels hit the runway." So many of us like to have one last drink; he was no different.'

When she discovered where he was, Michael's mother Margaret made an emotional appeal to her son to get in touch with her. Close to tears, the 79-year-old told the same newspaper: 'Drinking, pills, an unhappy childhood... I'm absolutely shattered to hear this.

'He must have been brainwashed to believe he had a bleak childhood. He is just making excuses for the drinking and the pills. He was a loved child, a happy child. He was the centre of the family. Everything revolved around him. This has almost broken my heart.'

Margaret, it turned out, eked out her life on a £65-a-week pension in the same south London flat where she had brought up Michael. She still treasured letters he had written from abroad when he was touring with his rock band. One began: 'Dear mum, hope you are well, miss you so much.' It ended: 'Your loving son.'

A month after he checked into Ashley House, Michael was back in Britain and raring to go. 'I know and understand the disease that's been eating at my sanity for years,' he insisted. 'I arrived at the clinic one month ago looking for something – and I found me. I've been humbled by the experience and the community of people from all walks of life. There was little contact with the world outside and I had no idea how people at home would react. They have responded with encouragement and love. I'd like to thank all my fans for their support.

'I've never allowed my condition to affect my ability to perform,' he insisted. 'When I'm seen performing live or on television, the comment is often made, "What's he on?" At no time has there been any substance whatsoever. And at no time has my marriage to Cheryl been in question. It is stronger now than ever. It is for Cheryl's sake and my own that I came here. I am giving me back to Cheryl and to the people who accept me for what I am.'

So, he was covering up as usual. His honesty about his alcohol problems was a brave step, but he was still not willing to stretch to an admission of his homosexuality. Although he was never high when he went on stage, Michael was no stranger to 'substances'. And his marriage to Cheryl was anything but strong.

But he had his defenders. From America, Father Joseph Martin paid tribute to the troubled comedian: 'Michael is an extraordinary man with a gigantic talent. We've been impressed by the fact he is so ordinary and genuine. He captured the hearts of everyone here, not only the staff but also fellow patients.'

Television bosses stood by him too and he opted to stay with LWT for a reported £5 million. 'He's the top light entertainer in the country,' said John Fisher, then head of variety at Thames Television, 'it's a position Bruce Forsyth held fifteen years ago and Max Bygraves held in the Fifties.'

Michael also decided to do a limited summer season at Blackpool after all. 'I should have been back last week,' he said as he arrived back in Britain from the clinic. 'I'm going to have to work twice as hard to be ready to open next week.'

When he did open, in front of a 3,000-strong audience at Blackpool Opera House, he seemed to perform better than ever before. Everyone in the audience knew of his recent troubles and everybody seemed determined to welcome him back. Michael received a standing ovation before he even said a word. And then he was into his stride. 'I'm awight!' he cried to more roars of approval, before adding, 'Thank you for making this a night to remember. There's been a lot I've forgot.'

Michael seemed determined not to hide his problems that night. At one point, a woman came in to view, walking down the aisle – always a mistake at a Barrymore show. As usual, he pounced. 'Where are you going, love?' he asked. 'I'm lost,' she said vaguely. Michael replied, 'Yes, love. I was too, for five years.' Then he hauled her on to the stage and kept her there until her husband sped down to the front to reclaim her – at which point Michael began behaving like a lover caught in the act.

The audience loved it. All the favourites gags were back: Michael started throwing people out again, one for looking like Rumpole, and one because he was Garry Bushell, then television reviewer for the *Sun* (and a great Barrymore fan).

Garry sneaked back in, only to be thrown out again. He crept back a third time, at which point Michael grabbed his notebook. 'He came on stage stoned out of his mind,' Michael read jokingly, before adding: 'Last time I saw you, Garry, you were disguised as a tree' – a joking reference to the reporters who had tried to interview him while he was at the US clinic.

Then he was off again, wrestling with grannies and announcing at the end of the show: 'Everyone over to the wine bar now – drinks are on me.' As he sipped a glass of orange juice on stage, he remarked: 'This is nice, I'd better get used to it.'

Sadly he didn't get used to it. But Blackpool was the performance of a lifetime, according to the critics, and Michael was rewarded with a five-minute standing ovation. 'It was a better buzz than I've ever had before,' he enthused after the show. 'Just to see all the people standing up was very emotional for me, and everyone backstage as well. If this is indicative of the way the country feels, then it gets rid of all the fear.'

It was exactly the way the country felt. 'His show was a dazzling display of a man at the top of his form,' wrote the late Jack Tinker in the *Daily Mail*. 'The man is the most dearly loved performer currently headlining in Britain today. His problems are our problems. His joys are ours, too.'

Pauline Wallin in the *Today* newspaper was equally fulsome in her praise. 'Last night in Blackpool, the love affair with the public was stronger than ever,' she said. And from David Lister, a little more haughtily in the *Independent*: 'The delivery, timing, facial expressions and astonishing audience rapport showed him to be something out of the ordinary. It was impossible not to laugh, even if one was slightly surprised to be laughing.'

Yet off stage Michael's triumph was to be qualified by a huge sadness. It was while he was in Blackpool, signing autographs on the way out of the theatre, that he fell headlong into another trauma... news that his father was dead.

A friend of Michael's revealed: 'Michael was such a huge hit at Blackpool that there were always crowds outside the stage door. His driver would bring the car as close as possible, but it always took ages for Michael to get through the mass of bodies because he stopped to sign so many autographs. Also, he could never just scrawl a signature, he'd have to chat and swap a joke or two. It was his way of extending the high he got from a performance.

'Even when he got into the car, the driver couldn't put his foot down because there were still fans clamouring at the windows for yet more autographs.'

As he jotted his name on the outstretched scraps of paper and programmes, Michael didn't notice someone talking to the chauffeur on the other side of the car. There was always something going on and he could only concentrate on one thing at a time. It was left to that driver to break the news to Michael that his father was dead.

'I didn't really take it in,' said Michael later. 'I thought, I can't believe what he's saying.' But a letter from his mother, even though they still weren't talking at this time, confirmed the news. His father, it turned out, had died some six years before. A Page 1 newspaper report spelled it out in grim terms: 'Barrymore's dad dies in pauper's grave'.

What astounded Michael most was the realisation, based on his own experiences of excess, that his dad had suffered from a disease. 'If you've got it, it's a lifelong disease, of alcoholism and gambling – in his case, compulsive gambling,' he said, his eyes clouded with sorrow.

Though he knew it would never be read, Michael sat down and wrote a letter to his dad, pouring out feelings that had altered as he had matured, feelings he was only just coming to terms with. He wrote that he understood the disease, that he was sorry he hadn't been able to understand it sooner, and that he was desolate that he had been consumed with such hatred. Then he put away his pen and once again found solace in the only way he knew how… by working.

His *Barrymore* show and the final series of *Strike It Lucky* were screened in the autumn and he was praised as never before. 'We have a long-term contract with Barrymore,' said John Kaye Cooper of LWT. 'We have him under contract for another three years and wish it could be twenty. He's a unique entertainer – the people's performer. He brings out the best in guests and never attempts to outshine them.'

Steve Leahy, head of entertainment company Action Time, was equally impressed. 'He combines on-screen charisma with off-screen charm,' he said. 'It's a trick few hosts can pull off. There are some who are a bundle of laughs with the contestants when the cameras are running, but not so great when they stop. Viewers may think it looks easy to host a game show, but it's one of the most difficult jobs in television – and it's certainly one of the most demanding.

'Often a number of shows are recorded one after another. There's tremendous pressure. Barrymore just takes it in his stride and manages to keep the studio audience happy despite all the stopping and starting during the recording. He's up there with veterans such as Bruce Forsyth and Bob Monkhouse.'

Nor was Michael afraid to talk about his problems on his shows. One of the first guests on the new series of *Barrymore* was Father Joseph Martin, the Roman Catholic priest who had helped him in the Ashley House rehabilitation centre. 'This man is a national treasure,' commented Father Joseph.

The rest of the country thought so too. They rushed out in

droves to buy Michael's new video, *The Unpredictable Michael Barrymore Live*, as the BBC yet again tried to tempt Michael to switch sides.

His legendary rapport with his young fans was also stronger than ever. Fifteen-year-old Sarah Hartshorn was a chorus girl in 'Cinderella', but she had been viciously attacked by a pair of brick-wielding girl thugs and left with two black eyes. She went to see Michael perform live, little realising that he knew she was there and had been told what she had gone through. He pulled her up on stage and presented her with a huge bunch of flowers. 'That was the best night of my life,' she said afterwards. 'Michael Barrymore has been my hero since I saw him playing Buttons in "Cinderella" when I was seven. I couldn't believe it when he invited me on stage. I felt so happy I burst into tears. It was a night I'll never forget.'

In December too he gave one of his most revealing interviews to the *News of the World*. 'Before I started the rehab course, I really thought I was going insane,' he admitted. 'Nothing seemed to make sense. I was happy being Michael Barrymore, oh yes I loved that, but I wasn't happy being Michael Parker. I didn't much like ME. Now I've cleared all the craziness out of my head and I'm happy being me.

'Learning that I had a disease called alcoholism was initially a great relief,' he revealed. 'You realise that it's something you're born with and it's not your fault. It's nothing to do with how much you drink. It's all about the reasons why you drink. You do it to try to change the way you feel.'

He admitted, 'The initial thing was for me to say, well, I had a rotten childhood. But that's got nothing to do with it really. It goes a whole lot deeper. You're born with it and it's going to be with you all your life. Addiction doesn't take holidays or days off. It doesn't discriminate between who it will and who it won't go for.

'People find it difficult to understand alcoholism. They see the dosser in the street with his can of beer or the bloke you don't want to sit near on the bus and they think that's it. I was in the clinic with men and women from all walks of life. Some with no money who'd been found under bridges, some middle-class people, lawyers and so on. Some very wealthy people. I had no special privileges. It was a very strict regime. We'd start early in the morning with lectures, talks, therapy sessions, until lights out at 10.30. There was no TV and no newspapers, except on Sundays. For the first time in my life I could talk freely about me. I went through emotions I had never experienced before.'

Speaking less than a fortnight later, he talked about his life with Cheryl, though he voiced none of his frustrations at living under her control. Indeed, if anything he stressed what a close-knit couple they were. 'When I was in the clinic I was away from Cheryl for a month,' he revealed. 'Before that, the longest we'd been separated was about a day. My disease is alcohol, her addiction's me.

'I haven't packed a case in eighteen years, or unpacked it. Not because I'm lazy. I just don't, she does it. I get up in the morning, my clothes are there. If I opened the cupboard, I wouldn't know where anything was.'

And recalling how they met, he added: 'I'd decided to go it alone in show business when suddenly this girl come along, nice face, and she was genuinely interested in me. I had teeth up here, naff suit on, no money and she asked, "How do you find so much enthusiasm?" And I said, "I just like it. I find it easier to live up there than I do down here." Which makes life difficult, because you can't stay up there twenty-four hours a day.'

Michael had put his finger on the biggest problem in his life, but the public face was still grinning. In 1995, he tempted 85-year old Chili Bouchier, one of cinema's earliest sex symbols and star of the 1936 film *Gypsy*, out of retirement and got her to sing a duet with him. 'I really didn't want to sing because I hadn't done it in public for five years, but I just couldn't resist Michael, he was too persuasive,' Chili confessed. He also persuaded four-year-old Zizi Langford – niece of the late Bonnie – to join him on stage and rounded off proceedings by throwing her off the stage and ten feet in to the orchestra pit. Zizi was unfazed. 'I wasn't nervous at all,' she smiled, 'I had lots of fun. Michael is lovely and funny. I wasn't scared when he dropped me from the stage – there was a man waiting to catch me.'

But there were also bad times in 1995. In February, Michael's mother-in-law Kitty Cocklin tragically died. The following month, extracts from his autobiography, *Back In Business*, were serialised in the *Sun*. In it, Michael told of his rise to fame and descent into alcoholism and admitted: 'Cheryl was addicted to me – but I was addicted to Jack Daniel's.' Michael provided an intimate diary of his time in America at the Ashley Clinic and stated that he couldn't have 'won' his battle against booze and drugs without Cheryl's help.

Elsewhere in Michael's autobiography, Cheryl told how her own weight dropped to 6 stone as she feared her husband had given up the will to live. She also launched a bitter attack on Michael's family for, as she said, 'betraying' him with press interviews. 'Michael was just a meal ticket to them,' she fumed.

In April, Michael's sister Anne called on her mother and brother to end their feud with him. 'I love my brother and I haven't got a bad word to say about him,' she said. 'And nor should my mother or brother. The picture they've painted of him is a fantasy as far as I'm concerned.'

Anne, a mother of two who lived with her printer husband Colin in a council house in Penge, south London, was clearly intent on smoothing over the troubled family waters and getting her loved ones back on speaking terms. 'I don't blame my mum,' she maintained. 'She is old, hard of hearing and her mind gets confused. She remembers things that didn't happen and forgets things that did. My mum has made it sound as though I was upset that Michael didn't come to visit me in the week I was in hospital for the operation [Anne had had a mastectomy operation two weeks before the interview]. I think she said it in the hope of making him feel guilty. I was extremely upset. The op's not exactly something you want the world to know about and I only told a very few close friends about it.

'I didn't want Michael to know either,' she added. 'He has problems of his own and I didn't want to add to them. I feel that I'm being used as a stick to beat Michael with and that's the last thing I want.

'He's been great to my family over the years. I can't thank him enough for that. He's given us money and treated our kids like his own.'

Anne's picture of Michael was a long way from the one painted by his mother and brother. 'Michael was always someone I could rely on,' she said. 'On my wedding day, John was meant to be giving me away. But he was late and Michael stepped in, although he was only sixteen. I was so proud of him – he saved the day. Michael was always the apple of my mum's eye, but John was always getting into scrapes.

'When Michael came along, it put John's nose out of joint. Michael was always fantastic with my kids. So was his wife

Cheryl. They came to visit at least once a week. Michael would always turn up with a treat. He knew we were hard up, so he would buy the kids clothes and shoes. He bought Nicola a mountain bike for her seventh birthday.

'Often Michael would turn up at the house carrying bags of shopping – at least a week's worth. He would just plonk them on the floor and start playing with the kids. He never made a song and dance about it. My mum never went without either. I remember clearly that Michael regularly sent her money. Even when he was getting well known he never forgot us.'

'I also remember that when he was playing Aladdin in panto he gave me twelve free tickets. It was one of the high spots of my life. After the show Michael took me backstage. He introduced me to Frank Bruno and Gary Wilmot. He wasn't at all ashamed, though I did think he might be – you can't help thinking things like that when you aren't used to the high life. But he went out of his way to make me feel at ease. At the end of the evening he gave my kids £50 each. That's more than either of them have ever seen in their lives.'

Anne also bitterly regretted her involvement, a year earlier, with the *Sunday Mirror* interview in which both her mother and brother had painted a grim picture of Michael as a celebrity who had forgotten all about his family. 'I didn't want anything to do with the story,' she stressed. 'I was disgusted by the whole idea. I haven't talked to Michael since then. I was too nervous to ring him – I wouldn't have known what to say to him. I didn't want to get involved, to take sides. I felt it was best just to let sleeping dogs lie. I realised Michael had his problems and I had mine. I also knew he was very, very busy. I didn't blame him at all for not getting in contact, he must have thought he couldn't trust anybody, not even his own family.

'Of course I'd love to see Michael again – he's my brother and I love him,' she admitted. 'I know that if I were to pick up the phone and tell him I was in trouble he'd help. But I wouldn't do that. There's plenty of time for us to talk to one another once John and my mum stop sticking the knives in. All I hope is that Michael is happy. He worked like a slave to get where he is and deserves everything he's got – and more.'

If his relationship with his family was strained, Michael's marriage was in crisis – though he and Cheryl still presented a united front in public. In May 1995 Michael went missing for three days after a blistering row with Cheryl. He 'cracked' after hosting a televised VE Day spectacular in front of the Prince of Wales.

Two months on, just weeks after claiming he had beaten the bottle, the *News of the World* revealed Michael had booked himself back into the Priory for a new battle against alcoholism. He spent five days there. Soon after, Cheryl was seen leaving home with five large suitcases.

*Top left*: An early photograph of Michael with his family – including the mother whom he loved so much, and the father who caused him so much pain. Michael is in his father's arms.

*Top right*: Michael with his sister Anne at her confirmation.

*Bottom*: The wedding of Michael's brother, John. Michael is second from the right.

*Top left*: Michael in 1966.

*Top right*: Michael with his sister Anne on her wedding day in 1968. Michael is 16 years old in this picture.

*Bottom*: Michael with his mother Margaret, at his wedding to Cheryl.

Michael and Cheryl's wedding day, 10th June 1976.

Michael with Cheryl at various stages of their precarious marriage…

It took many years for Michael to come to terms with his sexuality. He is pictured here with his boyfriend Paul Wincott (*top left and bottom*); and (*top right*) Michael's lover, John Kenney.

Michael with some of his celebrity friends: Frank Bruno (*top left*); Anneka Rice (*top right*) – they were joint winners of the Rear of the Year award in 1986!; racing motormouth John McCririck (*bottom left*); and sharing a cuddle with Cilla Black (*bottom right*).

Funnymen together. (*Top*) With Ernie Wise and Frank Carson, and (*bottom*) with Roy Hudd.

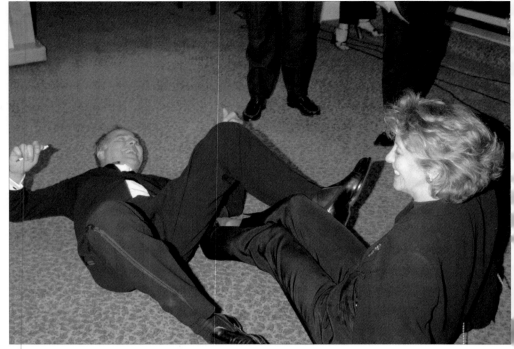

Michael in three very different poses! (*Top*) Drunk on the floor at the restaurant awards in London; (*bottom left*) on stage with a member of the audience in 1993; and (*bottom right*) Michael indulging in his characteristic tomfoolery in 1983…

# 11

# 'I HAVE A MENTAL ILLNESS, THE DISEASE TAKES OVER MY MIND'

'IT'S INSANITY,' says Michael, in what amounts to the most honest description of his problems that he's ever managed. 'Insanity is where I go to with drink or drugs, it's all OK with drink or drugs. Take that out of the equation, you can see the insanity.

'It will always come back to the disease,' he sighs, 'the disease will always tell me it's fine to do what I'm doing, it will have nothing to do with being correct, being nice or being sensible. That doesn't bear well with the disease, the disease has no regard for it, it doesn't care.

'And when the disease takes over in my mind, I can only speak for me, it tells me that what I'm doing is perfectly OK. That it's fine to be slowly killing yourself, to destroy yourself mentally... Alcoholism and drug addiction is a disease of the mind... If you want to call it mental illness and it's caused by having a drink or a drug and that's the label it has to have, then it doesn't bother me. I'd accept that totally, if that has to be the label then that's what I've got.'

Though he can see that now, he felt vulnerable and alone when Cheryl left. On stage, he kept looking into the wings for that familiar face. But now Cheryl wasn't there to smile back encouragement, to offer that nod of the head to show that a carefully worked routine had gone perfectly, just as planned and exactly as they'd worked it out sitting up in bed.

And as he filmed a new series of *My Kind of People* in Croydon, south London, Michael was alone in front of 10,000 people. It was the first time his wife and manager hadn't been by his side. As he walked on to the stage, the 43-year-old comic told the screaming crowd: 'I don't know what this show is about. I'll make it up as we go along – just like my life, really.' Then he broke into a dance, those long legs and big feet in highly polished loafers moving almost impossibly in perfect rhythm to a version of D-Ream's huge hit 'Things Can Only Get Better'.

But things were about to take a turn for the worse. And as one of his closest pals at the time revealed, booze was behind it all again: 'He was drinking more and taking more drugs, nothing anyone could say to him would make him stop. You'd start a conversation and he'd say, "Hang on, just let me get another drink and I'll be right with you." To say it was exasperating would be an understatement.

'It must have been terrible for Cheryl when they were together. Michael once told me that he'd always drink Coke from a can, not a glass, so no one could see how far he'd keep topping it up with Jack Daniel's.' And it wasn't just the demon drink that Michael was abusing: 'I think he knew he was wrecking himself, but he didn't seem to care. You could tell him, "Michael, taking drugs is illegal, it's against the law, do you understand?" But he didn't have to go to some street corner and buy stuff, it was always available in the clubs he went to and he didn't see what the problem was if he was only harming himself. You'd try to tell him that by supporting dealers he was supporting an industry that was killing his young fans, but the state he was in he couldn't reason that far ahead. Strangely, though, he could still think like lightning on stage, up there he really was a different person.'

By the summer of 1995, Cheryl and Michael were once more together – she had given him another chance. But around that time, a number of newspaper reports surfaced that would cause them both a lot of anxiety. Michael's brother John, hearing that Cheryl had walked out but not that she had returned, had gone on record with some hard-hitting words: 'As far as I'm concerned,' John said, 'it's goodbye and good riddance to her.

She's been nothing but trouble for him. Now she can go and jump off Tower Bridge with a brick around her neck to make sure she doesn't come up again.'

John, who had not seen his brother for eleven years, said Barrymore 'didn't stand a chance' against Cheryl. 'She's a very strong woman, very domineering.' he added. 'He's always been weak, a bit of a wimp.'

More surprisingly, a drunken Michael let his heterosexual public mask slip for once, when he tried to seduce fellow TV comedian Bobby Davro in a moment of madness. He lurched into Bobby's hotel room in Birmingham and suggested they spend the night together. Bobby, who is strictly straight and had recently married, was aghast and ordered Barrymore to leave. Giving Michael the benefit of the doubt, he put the incident down as just another Barrymore prank. But the revelation of what happened that night led friends to talk openly for the first time about the gay secret that was clearly on the verge of coming out.

Drag queen Ricky Greene, who first got to know Barrymore when they were both struggling comics on the stag night circuit, revealed: 'I often told Michael that it would be a huge weight off his mind if he came out and that nobody would be bothered. But he was frightened the public would never accept it and he'd lose everything he had.'

At last, though, the floodgates were starting to open. Next,

Michael's former personal assistant John Davis confessed to the *People* newspaper that he had twice had sex with his boss. It had taken place while Michael and Cheryl were on holiday in Florida. Davis had flown separately to the States for his own holiday, but the two men had met up for an outing. They found themselves staying away overnight – nothing new to Cheryl, who had now learned not to expect Michael – and were sleeping in the guest room of a mutual friend's house, where there were two single beds.

Davis revealed: 'We were both pretty drunk and I got into one bed and he got into another. I was just dozing when I suddenly realised he was lying on top of me and saying, "I want you." I tried to laugh it off at first, but then I kissed him back. He became amorous and I became more amorous and one thing led to another. We ended up having sex.'

Later, Davis visited the Barrymores' holiday home in Palm Beach. Michael sneaked naked into his room and slipped into bed with him. "We kissed and hugged each other and once again we made love," Davis revealed. 'Cheryl asked me a dozen times, "Is Michael gay?" but I've never been able to say "Yes."'

Davis, who later quit working for Barrymore because he was unable to cope with the comic's double life, clearly felt guilty about the indiscretions: 'I wish it hadn't happened – I've never slept with someone's husband before. And I never told Cheryl about what happened between me and Michael.'

Two weeks after Davis made his confession, Michael finally admitted he was gay. 'It had to come out,' said his pal. 'You couldn't be as famous as he was and expect every visit to a gay club to remain a secret. 'I'd been going out more and more to gay clubs,' Michael says now. 'I used to wear a baseball cap and I'm 6 foot 3 inches and pretty recognisable. People would lift up the cap and say, "Oh, it's you. What are you doing here?" 'I'd say, "Oh, I'm just out for the night." His pal added: 'There weren't many gays in London who hadn't seen Michael Barrymore in a club.'

# 12

# 'YOU'LL BE DEAD BY CHRISTMAS'

JUST A FEW weeks after Cheryl returned to him, Michael went for a medical check-up. The drink and the drugs were taking their toll. He admits now: 'I was trying to be treated for the mental state I was in and a doctor said to me, "I've had enough of all this, if you don't go out and do what you've got to do and be what you've got to be, you're going to be dead by Christmas."'

It marked a turning point in his private life. Michael knew he had to come out and openly confess his homosexuality. The night, when it came, had no advance publicity, though it was to be the most stunning Michael Barrymore show ever. It was the end of August 1995 and Michael had been invited to judge a 'beautiful boots' contest at the White Swan, a gay pub in east London.

Drag queen compere Dave Lynn introduced Michael to the audience and, more out of devilment than anything else, put the persistent gay rumours to him. 'Have you finally decided to tell the world?' he asked. The audience of about 200 went wild with anticipation.

Michael lapped up the cheers. He nodded, placed his hands on his hips and announced: 'Yes. It's time to tell the world… yes, I am.'

He then looked at his wedding ring, shouted 'F*** it' and launched into a version of the Frank Sinatra hit 'New York, New York', with the opening line amended to: 'Start spreading the news, I'm gay today.' Michael then told the audience: 'You're all invited back to my place – but you'll have to be out by three because the wife will be home.'

Compere Lynn, who wears a Bet Gilroy wig for work, recalled: 'I was gobsmacked to say the least.'

A member of the audience that night remembers every second of the evening's events. 'Someone told me that Michael Barrymore was in the corridor,' he said. 'Word went round and we were all straining for a look. Dave Lynn was up on stage and didn't know he'd arrived and started talking about all the gay stories that were going round about Michael. They were hilarious and we were laughing our heads off. Then Dave noticed that not everyone in the crowd was looking at him and asked, 'He's not here is he?' With that, Michael jumped on stage and said, "Yes I am, mate, what about it?" That's when Dave asked him to come out… and he did. He looked very happy.'

The *News of the World* reported the event on August 20. The day afterwards, Cheryl and Michael announced the breakdown of their eighteen-year marriage, though Cheryl said she would continue as Michael's manager. 'It was a massive blow for her,' said their pal. 'During the times when she couldn't deny, even to herself, that he liked men, she would insist that it was a fad and he'd get over it. She even told Michael, "We can work it out." It showed just how much she loved him. But they were never going to work this out. The gulf between them was too great and, more than anything else, Michael told me he felt free for the first time in his life. Not so much free from Cheryl, but free from the one secret that had haunted him throughout his life. Now he had a new existence and Cheryl couldn't be part of it.'

Two days later, Michael chose a 2 a.m. show hosted by gay DJ Jeremy Joseph on little-known Spectrum Radio to reveal his years of torment as a married homosexual. In an intimate conversation punctuated by laughter he shared his innermost thoughts. Michael admitted he had experienced homosexual feelings before marrying Cheryl but had hoped they would evaporate with time.

'We started off as best mates and we got married with the best intentions,' he revealed. 'Everybody does and I thought, like a lot of people, that the other feelings would just go away. Nineteen years ain't bad. Having said that, the situation with myself doesn't change what I owe her. We're too entwined, really. We've just separated for a while. I talk to her every day, we see each other and take it a day at a time. I've learned to stop looking over my shoulder, afraid of what people may or may not do or say.'

He continued: 'My life is an open book for millions of people. I decided that if I carried on I didn't think I'd be around for much longer because I was drinking to block how I felt or to give me courage. And then I'd get in a state and not really be in control. I decided it was time I wanted to take control of my life and think about ME for five minutes.' That said, he wasn't going to complain about the attention his fame had brought him: 'You can't spend twenty years in show business saying you want to be recognised and then when you are, say you don't like it. You can't put yourself on a pedestal and take all the glory and say the minute you come off, "Please don't bother me, this is my private life." So you have to do it with good grace.'

Michael insisted that he had not planned to come out at the White Swan. 'I didn't think about it,' he went on. 'I just stood up on stage and it went from there. The reaction was so enormous that they wouldn't let me down and the warmth that came across was unbelievable. I just went along with it. It was the best thing I've ever done. I never walked in there thinking I was going to say it and that this week would then turn out as it did. Having said that, if I went back to that time and had a choice I don't think I'd change it.

'It reminded me of when I started in the business and the pubs where I learned my trade. I used to get up in front of my friends and just make them laugh. I wanted to, not because I was earning a lot of money from it.'

And he had a word or two of advice to offer for closet gays: 'It's very difficult for a girl or boy to go up to their mum or dad and tell them what they think they don't want to hear. They get to my age or a bit more and they go, "I can't do it." But from the little experience I've had, it ain't as bad as you think.'

The admission that he was gay, though, was a body blow to at least one person – his mother Margaret, who at this time hadn't spoken to her son for five years. She had never guessed the truth about his sexuality. 'This has come as an absolute shock to me,' she admitted. 'It's like a bad dream. I can accept it, but I'd rather it hadn't happened. I didn't understand what was causing his drinking.' She added bravely: 'You're a mother first and last and nothing changes that. Hopefully he will get himself sorted out and live his life the way he wants it.'

However, Margaret's magnanimity did not extend to Michael's ex-partner. She blamed Cheryl for turning him against her: 'We were a perfectly happy family until they married,' she said. 'She saw his potential. Her exact words were, "Michael isn't yours now, he's mine."'

On August 28, Cheryl cleared Michael's clothes out of their home in Bayswater, but the following night, despite their traumas, she accompanied her husband to the National Television Awards. He won three trophies: Best Quiz Show; Best Entertainment Presenter (both for *Strike It Lucky*); and Most Popular Family Programme (for *Barrymore*). His acceptance speeches acknowledged both his fans and Cheryl for their support.

Fellow stars cheered Barrymore as he went on stage at Wembley Conference Centre to collect his awards. Michael joked: 'May I first apologise for the state of my suit. It's not the best one I have in my wardrobe. But the rest have been thrown out.' Prince Edward's girlfriend Sophie Rhys-Jones, who helped with PR for the event, was among the laughing onlookers.

On October 23, Michael sang 'I Am What I Am' at London's Royal Albert Hall as part of Stonewall's Equality 95 event. Then he rounded off the year in December by winning Best ITV Entertainment Presenter for the third year running at the British Comedy Awards. Again he arrived with Cheryl, but this time he had a trick up his sleeve. He unplugged host Jonathan Ross's autocue after he had lampooned other celebrities.

Two days later, Michael released a single called 'Too Much for One Heart', a song he wrote in collaboration with lyricist Don Black. It was a message of thanks to Cheryl for her support and reached number 25 in the charts. It was a year neither of them would ever forget.

# 13

# MY LOVER'S THE ONE WITH HIS PISTOL IN A HOLSTER

SHE MIGHT have been by his side at public events, but with Cheryl gone from his private life, the only serious constraint on Michael's darkest excesses was removed. 'And though he thought she was simply controlling him, he suddenly discovered that he really needed that control,' said a close pal. 'On stage he has the audience to give him certain boundaries to work in; off stage he needed those same strictures because without them he went wild. I know he thought that admitting he was gay would be the answer to all his problems, that he would settle down. But the opposite happened, he felt he had a licence to do all the things he'd forbidden himself from doing… at least too much.

'His drinking went off the scale and his drug taking followed.

Never when he was working, but as soon as the applause ended, as soon as he was off stage or off camera, he'd have a snort or take a swallow of Jack Daniel's. He even tried swallowing cocaine, trying everything because he could. There was no one at home for whom he'd have to make up an excuse. Everyone now knew he was off the rails, he was making headlines virtually every day so he simply played to that new audience and gave them what they expected... a wild man.'

During this time there were also more gay liaisons that ever before. Michael had embraced a promiscuous lifestyle, despite the dangers of a millionaire star meeting strangers and putting himself in vulnerable situations.

Meanwhile, Cheryl reacted to her star husband's partying by crying on the shoulder of the man she'd divorced over two decades earlier. Producer Greg Smith, the man behind the 'Confessions of... ' films, had parted from Cheryl after three years of marriage but they had remained firm friends.

Eventually Michael, now forty-three, started to stabilise too and began to openly date his first gay boyfriend. He had fallen for 22-year-old Paul Wincott, a waiter at London's Dorchester Hotel. Just a month after his gay confession, fans recognised Michael arriving at Paul's east London flat. Mind you, if he'd been trying to keep the date low profile, he probably shouldn't have turned up in his silver Bentley. Neighbours in the Chadwell Heath area were also fascinated by the fact that Michael arrived with a suitcase, two Selfridges bags and a painting.

After a trip to an Indian takeaway the pair then stayed in for the night. Early-morning passers-by noticed Michael leaving at around 6 a.m. Again, he was wearing his now-trademark off-screen uniform of sweater and baseball cap.

Everything looked hunky-dory until Michael took Paul to London's Heaven nightclub... and hugged the doorman. It was probably a bad move on an early date. A miffed Paul stormed off in tears, though eventually he and Michael made it up, returned to the club and danced until the early hours.

The pair eventually made a public declaration of their love in November 1995 – by posing as two US Confederate soldiers! They popped into Old Time Portraits in London's Piccadilly Circus for the Civil War photographs. In the bizarre picture Michael looked mean and moody, clutching a rifle in one hand and a bottle of Jack Daniel's in the other. Paul was behind him, his pistol firmly in its holster. Michael was so pleased with the snaps that he paid £40 for two copies.

Strangely, in January 1996, it was reported that Michael and Cheryl were to resume living together. Maybe because of this, plans for a New Year skiing holiday with Paul in the romantic Austrian village of Kitzbuhel went rapidly downhill.

Despite working at the five-star Dorchester, Paul insisted that he and Michael 'roughed it' on the winter break, so they stayed in the two-star Club Villa Hummer chalet with thirty-nine other guests, paying £423 each for the privilige.

As other revellers celebrated the New Year with drinks and dancing in the bar, he and Paul sat glumly in a corner together. A fellow skier recalled: 'On the biggest night of the holiday Barrymore kept a low profile. Some of us hoped he'd put on an act, but he scarcely stayed up past midnight. Every time he and Paul came into the bar they'd sit away from the rest of us and stare at each other for ages.

However, storm clouds were brewing even this early in the relationship. 'Soon they were having rows,' the fellow guest revealed. 'Every now and again Paul or Michael would storm off and we found them again down some little corridor at each other's throats.

'I can't even remember seeing him and Paul while the rest of us were shaking hands and hugging each other on the stroke of midnight. It would be nice to think they'd slipped off to celebrate the New Year in some intimacy, but difficult to believe. By the time everyone left for home, it was obvious they weren't a couple any more. It was sad.'

Back in London, Paul stormed out of the star's Bayswater home. The reports were correct, Cheryl had agreed to take him back. Michael left it to a friend to announce the news: 'The truth is, and this may astonish some people, they are sharing the same bed again.' Michael said later: 'I've never stopped loving her, not for a single day. I do want to be at home because that's where I feel safe. But I also get claustrophobic and I just have to get away on my own. There are times around the house when I dread even the phone ringing.'

A friend of the couple, recognising that Michael was once more torn between heterosexuality and homosexuality, chipped in: 'Poor Michael's really hit rock bottom. I don't know how Cheryl is going to rescue him this time."

It was a tough job indeed. On April 15, Michael complained about 'demons' in his mind that made him think his head was about to explode. 'It's like there are ten people talking inside your brain and you can't make any sense of it,' he explained. 'It felt like my head was going to pop and I was having to keep it under control with my hand. My brain jumps all over the place these days.'

Six days later he was at the centre of a drugs overdose riddle. Police and ambulance crews rushed to his west London home after receiving two frantic 999 calls shortly before 6 a.m. But after being warned to deal with a suspected drugs overdose, both crews were turned away at the door and told: 'Thank you, but everything is now all right.'

Fifteen hours after the ambulances left his home he appeared at the BAFTA awards ceremony in London's Theatre Royal. He seemed unsteady and left the audience, including Princess

Anne, cold with a string of unfunny gags. For once, Michael seemed ill at ease facing an audience.

A guest at the awards said: 'We weren't sure if he'd been drinking again, but there was obviously something very wrong. He was very rude, he was rambling and his eyes were beady and red. He seemed very delicate and Cheryl clung to his side all night. It was awful. He looked at his wits' end.'

Cheryl felt it was time to explain why she put up with it all. 'The past six months have been a living nightmare,' she said. 'There are times when I don't know how I've been able to cope, it's all been so tiring. I've never come closer to the edge. The only thing that has pulled me back is the fact that I love Michael very much. The separation was awful, just the worst thing I've ever been through. When you've been together like us for twenty years, it hurts beyond belief.

'You've got to understand that Michael is a man who's easily influenced, very easily influenced, by the people around him. Let me put it this way. Just a few months ago Michael was absolutely serious about joining a monastery. This wasn't some flippant idea but something he became obsessed with. He met a man at Alcoholics Anonymous who convinced him that if he was to find piece of mind he should live a monastic existence.

'He was perfectly prepared to put every penny he had earned into the religious group who were running it. You can't imagine the frustration of dealing with something like this. You try to tell them that it's ridiculous but they won't listen. Eventually I actually pulled out a kitchen knife and threatened him with it. That's when it dawned on Michael just how ludicrous it all was. He dropped the idea and it has never been mentioned again. It was forgotten, it was just another phase.

'No one can imagine how I felt when he announced he was gay. I now know what it means to be the "last to know". I certainly was. I've been through all sorts of stages with Michael, including one when he was influenced by the glamour of wide-boy thugs. I suppose it held a sort of romantic notion for him. But the gay thing, well, when I look at Michael I don't see a gay man and I should know. For heaven's sake, I've been with him for twenty years.'

By now Cheryl was well into her stride. 'The trouble with Michael is guilt,' she went on. 'He carries so much emotional baggage around with him. He feels enormous guilt about what he's done to me and I know he finds it hard to deal with. I wonder why I can't just walk away, but I couldn't leave him like this. I want him to be cured. I'm desperate for him to get help. There must be some way he can find happiness. God knows how often he has tried to "find himself". But nothing seems to work for long.'

Cheryl remained unconvinced that his frequent trips to

expensive clinics had actually helped Michael at all. 'It's easy, of course, to see things in retrospect,' she admitted, 'but I do regret the time he spent in the Ashley Clinic in America. He went because he was at a very low ebb and needed to sort himself out. What it did was to expose Michael to another extreme of influence. Unfortunately, I believe he was brainwashed into thinking that he was entitled to say and do just whatever he pleased. In effect, they told him that one has to be ruthless in the pursuit of finding oneself – even if that meant hurting other people. As for the drinking, well, for a while the clinic did straighten him out. I think having time to himself did him good. But he became another person who talked a different language. It works for a lot of people, but it didn't work for Michael.' But ironically, it seemed that rehab was another form of addiction that the troubled star couldn't kick. Just days after Cheryl's outpouring, Michael was at his worst again. He was admitted to Marchwood Priory suffering from stress, depression and exhaustion.

In early May, Cheryl was seen leaving their London home to visit him at the clinic so they could celebrate his 44th birthday together. After loading up her chauffeur-driven Bentley with presents and flowers she told a *News of the World* reporter: 'I'll wish Michael a happy birthday from the *News of the World* readers. He'll really appreciate it. He's been very ill.' Indeed, though the problems in his personal life were by now well known, Michael still commanded a great deal of love and sympathy from the public. Staff at Marchwood had been inundated with cards and gifts from well-wishers across the country.

While he was at Marchwood, Michael began to brood over an issue that he thought he had overcome: his desire to be a father. He cradled a five-month old girl named Chantal in his arms after learning that her mother had just died from a drugs overdose. And when he was told that the child would be taken into care, he insisted, 'I'll look after her. I'll adopt her.' When social workers arrived to take Chantal away he pleaded again that he wanted to keep her. One nurse, who does not wish to be identified, confirmed: 'It was a gesture straight from the heart. He was genuinely moved. It was one of the most heartbreaking scenes I've ever witnessed.' But adoption expert Dr Kathleen Osborne said Barrymore would have to be passed as mentally fit to cope before being allowed to adopt. Nothing came of his plea and the child was eventually looked after by foster parents.

Michael spent two months being treated at Marchwood. And when he got out, he went straight to Paul! Once more, neighbours in Chadwell Heath watched as he helped load Paul's bags into the boot of his £215,000 Bentley before they drove off together. The following month, July 1996, they were spotted on holiday together in Ireland. Michael was paying his first visit in twenty-six years to Belmullet, the village in County Mayo where his mother's family own a farm.

He later told the *News of the World*: 'My mum can give you some lip, but she does it in a classic Irish way. She was born in County Mayo on a farm that looks over the sea and was one of eighteen children. My Uncle Paddy still runs the farm and all the children are still alive. My grandmother lived to 103, so Mum and me should both have a long innings. It's good breeding.

'It's like going back in time when I go to the farm,' he continued. 'The door is always open. There are no locks. I've no idea how many nephews and nieces I must have, but loads of kids come round, sit down and stare at me. I'm very popular in Ireland. I did *My Kind of People* once in Dublin and had 55,000 watching. It was heaving and absolutely magic.'

The trip with Paul was Michael's first contact with any of his relatives for nearly seven years. His Uncle Paddy revealed: 'It was a great surprise when he turned up in his big Bentley with his friend. We certainly weren't expecting him. Of course, we knew who he was because we see his shows on TV.'

But on a more ominous note, Paddy also revealed that Michael was back on the booze. 'I took him out to the local with Paul and he seemed to enjoy himself,' he said, 'but he's a little too fond of the drink, I think. He had a lager then a Budweiser then a whiskey.'

On his return to London, the ever-changeable Michael declared his love for Cheryl once more! Paul was finally out of the picture. Cheryl had tears in her eyes as he serenaded her in a Soho street with an impromptu performance of 'I Don't Know Why I Love You But I Do'. She didn't really know why she loved him either.

**14**

# 'YOU CAN'T PARK THERE, YOU'RE BLOCKING PRINCESS MARGARET'

HE WAS the stressed-out King of Entertainment. She was the trouble-torn Queen of Hearts. And after Michael was admitted to Marchwood Priory for stress and depression in the spring of 1996, Princess Diana became one of his dearest friends.

Diana had met Michael and Cheryl at a number of charity and showbiz events. But Michael admits he was amazed when the princess sent him a message suggesting they might meet. 'I thought it was wind-up,' he said with a smile. 'But when I saw her sitting there in my house I couldn't believe how absolutely stunning she looked. It's unusual for women to get more beautiful as they grow older, but she just got better.

'I knew from the first conversation where she was coming from. She kept telling me, "You've got to do things for you.

You've got to do what's right for you and not be controlled by other people.'" It was exactly what he'd been telling himself, exactly what his doctor had been telling him.

Michael went on: 'Diana used to say, "I'm glad when you're in the papers because that keeps me out." It used to be her for the Royals, Gazza for football and I covered entertainment.'

That first meeting with Diana went well. She had told him to stay in touch and she made it clear that wasn't just a polite way of saying goodbye, she really meant it. Michael dearly wanted to see her again but his off-stage shyness took over. He said: 'I thought to myself, I won't impose on her too much.'

Then, one day, the phone rang. It was her. Not some lackey speaking on her behalf, but the Princess of Wales ringing for a chat. 'Why don't you phone me back?' she asked. 'We really should stay in touch.'

Michael grinned: 'I told her, "To be honest, I don't want to bother you." But she said, "Well, bother me."'

Over the next year Michael regularly visited the princess at her apartments at Kensington Palace. In return, she made cloak-and-dagger visits to his home. The year 1996 was a bad one for Michael. Besides his time at the Priory he was also taken to London's Cromwell Hospital following a nervous breakdown. It came as he was filming *Strike It Rich*, the follow-up to his hugely successful *Strike It Lucky*. In December, London Weekend Television scrapped the rest of the shooting schedule for his other show, *Barrymore*, to give him time to recover. Throughout that trouble-torn year, Diana became a shoulder to cry on.

'We met a lot,' recalled Michael. 'She really helped and became a great mate.' There were funny moments too. 'I remember I took the Bentley round to the Palace one day and parked it outside,' he said. 'Diana told me, "You can't leave that there. Margaret has to get in and you're blocking her gap up." Then she joked, "The Bentley's a bit flash, isn't it?" I replied, "What's flash about it, it's just big. It's plain."'

Michael hoped for better luck in the New Year, but 1997 began with another bout of mental instability and he was again admitted to a clinic for stress and exhaustion. He told a just a few close pals about the nightmare he'd been going through. 'The way he told it, he and Cheryl were over in Florida for January,' explained one of his friends. 'He was drinking more and more again, sitting at the lakeside virtually pretending to fish because he was so out of it. Then he'd walk back to the house and take out all his frustrations on poor Cheryl, shouting and yelling his head off. He never hit her, but he did smash up a fair bit of crockery. The place could look like a bombsite after one of his sessions.

'Eventually Cheryl had enough, so she called this clinic and this man came to take Michael away. He never said where it was, but it seemed to do him some good. When he eventually got home to London he seemed much calmer.'

One of the casualties of Michael's illness at that time was the indefinite shelving of his celebrity extravaganza, *Barrymore In Hollywood*. But by April he had made sufficient recovery to star in a new series of *Barrymore*. That relatively calm period in his life was to be shattered in September 1997 with the news that Princess Diana had been killed in a car crash in Paris.

Michael was devastated. Shaking with emotion, he revealed in an interview with the *News of the World*: 'It happened in the early hours of a Sunday morning and I was going to see her the following Wednesday. When I first heard about it I was in The Fridge, a nightclub in Brixton. A medic came over to me and said, 'Michael, we've got to get you out of here'.

'He took me to a set of stairs and looked at me. He had tears coming out his eyes and he said, "Diana's dead." I sank to the floor. I just felt, this is some sick gag someone's playing. It can't be right. I was only [sitting] with her the other day. I remember saying to her, "I'll see you after the weekend." I was numb that whole week, and so were most other people.'

Michael was invited to Diana's funeral. And he was so heartbroken afterwards that he broke down and left the country. 'I stayed locked up until the funeral, ' he recalled. 'The day of the funeral we were standing in the Abbey and when her brother, the earl, said what he did about his sister, I thought it had started to rain outside. Heavily. But it was a clear day. Then

I realised: it was clapping. It hadn't started in the Abbey, it came from the public outside. It came so forcefully that it washed right the way down to the front.

'I just broke down. I couldn't hack it. I just got on a plane and left the country. I'd found a great mate and a great influence in Diana and suddenly it was taken away. She had a quality that I like to think I have for others, but not for myself. I'm good with words but not when I'm talking about myself. People stop me and tell me about their problems. They think they can approach me and treat me differently from others in the business.'

In the aftermath of her death, Michael's friendship with Diana affected the life of one other person, her trusted aide Paul Burrell. Paul had first got to know Michael when he acted as an early go-between between him and Diana. Now, as he was helping to wind up her estate he had to endure false slurs about the state of his own marriage and malicious gossip about his friendship with Michael.

Speaking from London, Paul said at the time: 'My living arrangements have changed, but not because of reasons given in some newspapers. My wife Maria and our boys are back at home in a familiar territory with friends and family. And I join them at weekends. But it's no different to an MP or anyone else working in London. My marriage is very strong and my family are the most important thing in my life. Maria's a saint to still be with me after all we've been through.'

Isolated in his own grief, Michael could only wish that he had someone permanent to fall back on too. His relationship with Cheryl was once more coming apart at the seams.

# 15

# 'I'VE TAKEN THE UNHAPPINESS PILL'

SOMEHOW, MICHAEL and Cheryl struggled on through the spring and summer of 1997. She must have breathed a sigh of relief that his most notable performance was on stage and not off. At a Royal Gala performance Michael climbed a ladder to the Royal Box and ordered Prince Charles to pay attention.

'I shouted "Oi! at Charles to make sure he was watching,' Michael explained. 'He started playing up to it. He put his hands up and said, "Oh sorry." Then I said, "He's just written us a letter with a PS: next time I'll have a microphone in the box."

'There were stories he was upset, but he wasn't at all. I don't know who the lady was with him but she bent up laughing and I said, "She went down there quick."

'After the show, Charles asked me, "Why don't you do the

same things to my mother?" I replied, "I don't think so, do you?" He said, "Why not?" He also said, "I'm terrified about what you're going to do to me next."

'It was so different from my first royal show. Then it was me who was terrified. I just wanted to get through it. Now I push it as far as I can.'

Just as he pushed himself. Referring to his many clinic visits, he admitted: 'I thought the world had come crashing down on my head. I lost my way. I'd wander round thinking everything I'd worked for didn't mean anything. The nice home, the money – they're just quick fixes. They don't mend your head for you, not when you've taken the unhappiness pill.

'None of the clinics really worked for me. I was being pushed and pulled so many ways, I didn't have a mind of my own.' Then, referring to the lies that he had been telling the very people who were trying to help him, he went on: 'Because I'm basically a people pleaser I'd tell them [the doctors and psychiatrists] what they wanted to hear. As much as I tried to be ordinary and people would say, "We'll treat you as one of us", after a while I'd end up controlling it all, just doing what I do for a living. It was like *One Flew Over The Cuckoo's Nest* in there. I'd arrange nights out and tours and get away with it. It didn't mend me.'

Nor could anything, ultimately mend his marriage. The showbiz pages on September 16, 1997 had a familiar ring to

BARRYMORE

them: 'Barrymore Splits From Wife Again'. So, everyone thought, he goes off the rails once more, then she'll take him back again. Why the hell does she do it?

This time, though, it was different. First, Michael's closest friends admitted that even he was rationally coming to terms with the fact that his marriage was finally over. And 'rational' wasn't a word you normally used to describe Michael Barrymore. 'He and Cheryl have been desperately trying to save their marriage for some time,' said one close pal. 'But nothing has been the same between them since Michael came out and admitted he was gay. He really wanted everything to work out, but it was increasingly clear their relationship had lost its sparkle.' (That was putting it mildly!) The pal added: 'Everyone's very saddened and concerned about Michael. He's very depressed at the moment, particularly due to the death of Princess Diana. She was his friend.'

Still, that autumn Cheryl dutifully turned up with Michael at the National TV awards. After all, she was still his manager. The couple arrived at the ceremony at London's Royal Albert Hall, putting on a brave show for the cameras. They were kissing and cuddling, full of smiles. Michael was getting a trophy for Most Popular Entertainment Presenter and Cheryl was determined to put on at least a show of unity.

But the evening was not destined to pass off smoothly. And the moment that he stepped up for his award will live in TV history, and in the memories of the 5,000 VIP guests. To start with, he appeared drunk. Again. And he cried. And even by his standards his acceptance speech was one of the most bizarre ever.

'It's not been a very easy time over the past couple of years,' he said, with a gift for understatement rarely matched in showbiz circles. Then, his voice shaking, he grabbed the lectern and went on: 'I really don't know what to say for once in my life.' His eyes darting wildly around the auditorium, he continued: 'Oh God, I felt awight when I came in!... Er, I'm the happiest I've ever been – but when you go through... and I know lots of families go through this kind of thing, but it's actually public...'

He tailed off, before starting again. 'I actually don't mind that, I've pushed the boundaries, I admit. I've sometimes gone over the top and things. But I'm a lucky something. All that fame and fortune bring you is fame and fortune but that doesn't stop you being a human being.'

By now the tears were rolling down his cheeks. 'I'm making a right "p" of myself now,' he said, a tremor in his voice. 'I was talking to the parents of the Safeway kid earlier [a child who had appeared in some Safeway adverts] and they said he wants to be me. I hope I'm not a bad example. If you've suffered what I've suffered recently... I spilled a gin and tonic and I've had nightmares about it.'

Just in case the assembled VIPs were in any doubt, Michael finished with: 'I don't know what the hell I'm saying.' Then he stepped backwards, held up his award and left the stage to applause.

Later, Michael drank champagne at a £50,000 after-show party in Kensington and admitted he had 'totally lost it' during his speech. 'It may have been a combination of being tired, or the emotion of the circumstances of my home life,' he shrugged. 'I've never lost control or broken down in front of an audience before, or even in private. I just think I didn't hold it together for the pure reason that I was totally lost for words to thank the public for supporting me.'

Then, speaking of Cheryl, he admitted: 'We are separated. Our marriage is over. We are separated not as best friends and not as business partners. I can't live a lie any more. I don't want to live a lie any more. I don't want not to be a friend of Cheryl's any more. I don't want her not to be my best mate.'

Intimating that he had a new boyfriend, he added: 'I'm fed up with lying about this because it does me no good and it does my partner no good.' When a reporter asked him about his partner, he replied: 'You don't think I'd tell you about him, do you?'

Michael went on: 'I've never had a problem with my work. What I have a problem with is accepting praise. I've decided for once in my life to be honest, that's the best cure – and if people don't like it so be it.'

That's probably just how Cheryl felt. Just seconds after he had walked off stage following his garbled acceptance speech she had hit the roof. When a female television executive approached Michael to congratulate him, Cheryl screamed 'F*** off!' at the startled woman, then went home alone.

Michael's speech was heavily cut before it went out on TV, but after reading his after-show comments in a series of newspapers the following morning, Cheryl announced she was filing for divorce, whether Michael saw the need for it or not. She revealed that Michael had become more and more depressed since the death of Princess Diana, but that whatever the motivation, she could take no more of his outrageous behaviour. 'I walked away because I couldn't bear to see him up there yet again crying his eyes out,' she said. 'I don't want to see him like this, but he can't stop doing it. The public want him to be a comedian, not some kind of sad, tear-stained man, full of unhappiness. I can't take any more of this. I need to find a life of my own in the same way that Michael appears to be doing.'

'The evening started so well,' she continued, with a sigh. 'We met at our home in Bayswater to get dressed for the ceremony and everything was brilliant. When we arrived everyone was shouting and screaming for us, and it was almost like the old times. We sat next to each other and Michael genuinely didn't know he'd won an award. It was a surprise to both of us. All he had to do was say thank you for the award, make a joke and sit down. But he couldn't do that – that was much too simple. This was his stage, his platform and he couldn't resist pouring out his heart to the world.

'People love and respect Michael because he's one of them, a grass-roots comedian, not because he's bursting into tears all the time. Of course I still care about him – especially when he's in this kind of state. He's been worse since the death of Princess Di, which seemed to set him back. I don't want to see him like this, wrecking the whole of his life, but he seems determined to press the self-destruct button.'

When he heard that Cheryl was filing for divorce, Michael too laid himself bare and made it clear that though he had 'come out' in the White Swan, even he had not fully accepted he was completely gay… until now.

'I know my marriage is over,' he admitted. 'I'm gay – it's no use pretending any more. The fact is, you can't beat nature. There are no easy or convenient ways around this. There are no other routes to take.'

But talking about Cheryl with obvious warmth, he added: 'I'm resigned to the fact that I'm losing the best friend I ever had. It's a terrible tragedy but I don't believe I've done anything that's wrong. I've got to deal with it. It's not a case of me falling out of love with Cheryl in any way whatsoever; if I didn't love her, none of this would matter to me. I wouldn't be talking like this in an honest, open manner. The truth is, I don't know how I've held out for so long. All I want to do is find some happiness instead of living this kind of artificial life.

'I ain't the brain of Britain,' he went on. 'I find it difficult to put into words what I genuinely feel – and often my honesty gets me into trouble. I'm not saying, "I'm all right Jack, shove you." Cheryl deserves all the happiness in the world and I will do everything I can to help her achieve that. I've never seen the need for a divorce, but I can understand the pain she's going through. I'm very, very hurt and conscious of the hurt I've caused her. I feel terrible for causing all this anguish.'

Drawing a deep breath, Michael added: 'The truth is that once words come out of your mouth you can't turn the clock back. You can feel guilty, but the damage is done. She's lost her husband, her lover and her work. There seems to be no need for all that pain but unfortunately that's the way it has to be.'

By now news had got out that the new man in Michael's life was a 24-year-old called Steve Platts. Steve and Michael were staying together in a rented flat in London's Docklands while Cheryl remained at the couple's Bayswater home.

Michael smiled: 'The truth is I am happier than I've ever been in my life. It's a massive relief to me that people know exactly what I am and can judge me for themselves. I fully accept today that my marriage is over and that I am gay. If I don't come to terms with this I'll carry on hurting people unnecessarily forever. You have to learn in your life that your career, even when you're someone like me, doesn't come first.

'I'm fed up with being the subject of dinner-table talk,' he continued. 'Anybody who says I stage-managed my awards speech is talking cobblers. Everything I say, I say from the heart, because that's the only way I know. All I'm trying to do is find some happiness. I know I lost it in my speech but I couldn't help it because that's the way I feel and the way I am. You can't go on pretending you're something you're not. I cannot go on any longer keeping up the pretence.'

But he admitted that to forge a happy new existence would be far from easy. 'You can't suddenly cast off such a large part of your life,' he added. 'I've been in rehab clinics and sometimes I honestly wonder how I can carry on.' In December 1997 the legal proceedings for divorce started. By the following May the marriage would be well and truly over, and Michael had signed a reported £1.5 million settlement.

During the run-up to the divorce, Michael had also been busy filming a cameo role in the Spice Girls' debut movie *SpiceWorld*, which opened nationwide on Boxing Day, 1997. He played a sergeant major-like dance teacher who had to put the girls through their paces at a military-style training camp.

'It was like *The Krypton Factor* on acid!' said Geri Halliwell. 'We were all in combat greens. Mel B looked like she was Public Enemy No.1 but she was Scary Spice on the swing jump. Emma was Private Benjamin and totally going for it. I looked like a cross between an old hippy and Rambo. Victoria wore a little green army dress and attempted the assault course in high heels – I don't think so!'

Mel C added: 'One of our in-jokes from the film came from the Michael Barrymore sketch, where he keeps saying, "That is correct." We like that one and use it quite a lot now.'

Mel B chipped in: 'It was great doing the assault course with Michael. At one point we had to swing across some water. We weren't supposed to end up in the stuff, but of course we did.'

In December too, Michael showed that he had lost none of his legendary appeal with his loyal fans, when the *News of the World* joined forces with the charity When You Wish Upon A Star, which organises celebrity treats for sick children. Curtis Chandler's greatest hope was to meet his idol, Michael. The seven-year-old from Nottingham suffered from Duchenne Muscular Dystrophy and two years earlier had been fitted with splints to help him walk. But the discomfort was forgotten when he was told he'd be having lunch with Michael at London's Planet Hollywood.

Curtis beamed as Barrymore walked in with a sack of presents, including huge toy trucks and colouring books. 'All my friends think I'm famous because I've met Michael,' said Curtis, his eyes shining. 'He's great.'

It was exactly the kind of situation in which Michael could

shine. But he put on another less than successful performance when he and Steve Platts made their first public appearance together in February 1998, attending the Challenge TV Game Show Awards at London's Savoy hotel. After a few glasses of champagne Michael took to the stage to collect Best Game Show Host and Best Game Show award for *Strike It Lucky*. Guests were treated to another bizarre spectacle, when he responded to a heckler who shouted, 'I love you', by yelling back, 'I love you too.' He added: 'That's gonna make tomorrow's papers, isn't it.'

Then he tore into the ceremony's host Bob Monkhouse for using an autocue. 'Fancy a chat without it being scripted?' he asked one of the great ad-libbers in showbiz.

Then, in a half-humorous remark that once more revealed his personal fragility, Michael said of himself: 'This is a common or garden game show host who's currently out of his trolley. I'd like to thank everyone for putting up with me and Bob. We are, in fact, two used car dealers from Romford.'

As he left the stage, a relieved Bob Monkhouse remarked: 'There's no one else anywhere like Michael Barrymore, someone who's willing to walk the gangplank without knowing if the ship is there.'

Michael, meanwhile, staggered into the press room where he blamed his behaviour on 'nerves'. Then he lay down on the floor, clutching his two trophies.

The caring side of Michael Barrymore. (*Top*) With young Sally Slater at the
Children of Courage awards at Westminster Abbey in 2000. Sally has a rare condition
called cardiomyopathy. (*Bottom*) At the funeral of Princess Diana. Diana was a
close friend of Michael's.

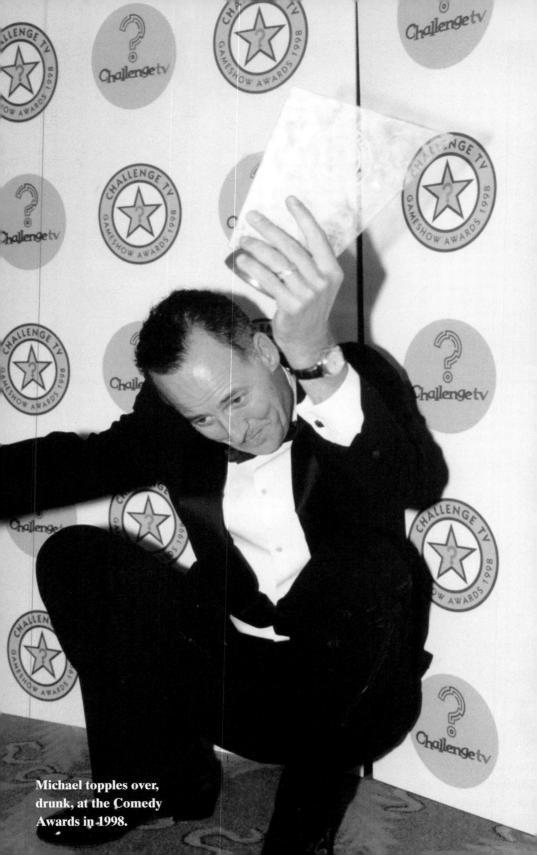

**Michael topples over, drunk, at the Comedy Awards in 1998.**

*Top*: Michael with his mother, whom he took to the National TV Awards in 2000, soon after they had become reunited.

*Bottom*: Michael trying to start his classic motorbike outside the grounds of his Roydon mansion; when the bike wouldn't start, his chauffeur arrived in a Mercedes to give him a push – but Michael ended up returning home in the car while the chauffeur was towed behind on the bike.

*Top*: A grim-faced Michael leaves the Middlesex Hospital after visiting his ill mother.
*Bottom*: Tearful Michael at his mother's funeral.

Stuart Lubbock, the young man found dead in Michael Barrymore's pool. (*Inset*)
Justin Merrit, who was also questioned by the police over Lubbock's death.

The day Michael Barrymore's life changed. After the death of Stuart Lubbock, police were stationed outside Michael's house, as he was taken to Harlow Police station for questioning.

Despite everything, Barrymore remains one of the country's best-loved entertainers. Here he clutches an armful of comedy awards – gestures of appreciation from an admiring public.

The following month, Michael hit the headlines again. A sickened mother told how she had welcomed Michael into her home, only for him to make sexual advances to her two sons and their teenage cousin. He had apparently cuddled up to eighteen-year-old Emerson Ford as the good-looking lad slept in his bed. He had also tugged at the clothes of Emerson's 21-year-old brother Simon and begged their cousin Darren, eighteen, for a kiss.

'He knew none of them was gay,' said 41-year-old Sylvia Ford, 'but he tried it on with them anyway. He was offensive, embarrassing and arrogant. He walked round my house like he owned it.' Sylvia claimed that Michael had latched on to Darren and labourer Simon when they asked for his autograph at a gay nightclub in Leicester. The two young men and Sylvia, an out-of-work nurse, had gone there from a pub because it was one of the few places where they could get a late drink.

Darren, who worked as a football coach, commented: 'I was nervous because I didn't want people to get the wrong idea of why I was there. I was gobsmacked when I spotted Barrymore at the bar talking to a couple of young men. I'd always had a lot of respect for him, so I thought I'd go over and ask for his autograph. We struck up a conversation but he was pretty drunk. He was on Jack Daniel's and Coke and said he'd already had eleven. He had a glazed look on his face and after a while I realised he was staring at me.

'Suddenly, without warning, he ran his hand through my hair and asked if I'd like to join him in his hotel room. I said no and walked off with Simon.'

But Michael was said to have followed the two lads, and when the club closed at 2 a.m. pleaded with them to take him home for a nightcap. A friend was driving them home and Michael seized his opportunity and jumped into the car with them all. 'We couldn't very well push him out,' said Darren. 'But I covered my lap with newspapers. I told him I didn't want any problems with wandering hands. Still, a few minutes later, when no one was looking, he put his hand on my leg and whispered something in my ear. I didn't hear him properly. So he blurted it out for everyone to hear – he asked for a kiss! I pushed him away and told our friend to stop and drop him off. But Barrymore got really angry and started shouting about how much money he had.'

Darren finally took pity on the star, who was in Leicestershire filming a TV commercial, and let him came to his Auntie Sylvia's home anyway.

Simon recalled: 'By the time we got there, he'd given up on Darren and I'd become his target. Mum offered Barrymore a drink and he asked for whisky. She didn't have any, so she gave him brandy and Babycham; there was only a little left. He didn't notice the difference and knocked it back in one.

'I went upstairs to the loo and he followed me. When I came

out he was waiting. He told me he needed to talk and ushered me into a bedroom. Then he asked me to shut the door and turn out the lights but I refused, so he shut it and then started pulling at my clothes.

'I pushed him away but he removed his jacket and asked if I wanted to take off a superstar's shirt. I told him he'd end up seeing stars if he made any more suggestions like that.'

Emerson, a trainee decorator, hadn't gone to the club, preferring to go to bed early because he had to attend a college course the following day. He said later: 'Mum had phoned from the club to tell me about Barrymore but I didn't believe her. Then I woke to see him poke his head round my door, then lay down next to me. I nearly jumped out of my skin.

'He stroked my leg through the blanket and mumbled something about everyone being bastards. I sat up and pulled the quilt around me. I only had my boxer shorts on and I was scared. I had visions of him trying to get into bed with me. Then I realised he was crying like a baby.'

The amazing scene took place only yards from where Simon's fourteen-year-old sister Kelly lay sleeping. She was woken by all the commotion and later overheard an astonishing exchange between Michael and his minder Chris, who had followed him to Sylvia's in a taxi.

The stunned schoolgirl explained: 'Barrymore seemed to be trying to tell Chris that he'd finished with a boyfriend called

Kevin – and now wanted him! Chris made it clear that he wasn't interested and this annoyed Barrymore, who started slapping Chris and shouting. Chris didn't retaliate, though, he just did his best to restrain him. What I remember most, though, was how tall Barrymore was – he had to duck to get through our door. And I've never seen anyone with such big feet. They reminded me of flippers.'

Barrymore's exchange with his minder was the last straw for mum Sylvia – she ordered him to leave. 'He sat down in a chair and put his head in his hands,' she remembered. 'He stayed like that for about five minutes. I think he was crying. I told him he must get help and he nodded in agreement.'

'We were flattered by the attention of a celebrity,' Sylvia said, 'but we just hope that the next time he complains about the way people treat him, he'll remember how he treated us. Although he's a comedian, he didn't make anyone laugh. My sons were shaken by the experience. It didn't take any of us long to realise that he was really screwed up. The real Michael Barrymore was nothing like the one on the box.'

A little over two months after Sylvia's description of their chaotic night, Michael and Steve Platts parted. Michael even took back a £50,000 silver Porsche he had bought Steve as a Christmas present... then he served a High Court writ, banning him from talking about their relationship or giving any details of his business affairs.

Heartbroken Steve fled to Las Vegas; his mother Diana accused Michael of being 'cold and callous'. Diana, who lives in Wilmington, Kent, summed up the effect the relationship had had on her son with one line: 'He wrecked Steve's life.'

Just days later, in June 1998, Michael was photographed out on the town with a new boyfriend – Shaun Davis.

# 16

# A GAY MARRIAGE IN HAWAII

SHAUN DAVIS was a 24-year-old barman plagued with debts when he met Michael at The Fridge nightclub in Brixton. It was the same venue that Michael had been in when he'd learned about Princess Diana's death.

Clearly sparks were flying from very early on between the two. Starstruck Shaun soon left his boyfriend, a chef named Kenny Hemple, quit his council flat and moved in with Michael. Just as Cheryl had done before him, Shaun gave up his job to devote himself to Michael and became his personal assistant. Looking back on those days, Michael now admits he wanted the same 100 per cent attention and commitment from Shaun as he had received from Cheryl. Shaun did have some work. He organised Michael's cue cards for his live shows.

In December 1998 Michael was named top ITV Personality at the British Comedy Awards. His ex-wife Cheryl, by now a free and independent woman, had fallen for a 23-year-old named Alex Rim. And as Michael picked up his award, he couldn't resist telling the world that both he and his wife had found toyboy lovers. Speaking at the London Television Centre, he joked: 'I've heard my ex-wife has found happiness with a new love and I'm thrilled. After all we've been through, she's now with a 23-year-old and at last, after twenty years, we've got something in common.'

But Shaun's own former partner, the now heartbroken Kenny, accused Michael of using his fame and wealth to seduce his boyfriend. He told how Michael had showered Shaun with gift after gift – including Armani suits and a BMW car. Kenny added morosely: 'He stole my lover and I despise him for it. Barrymore has turned his head and wrecked it all.'

The following March, Kenny must have been even more heartbroken when Michael and Shaun gushingly told of their love for one another in a newspaper interview. 'I've never been happier than I am now,' said Michael. 'And that's down to Shaun.'

By the summer, when Cheryl was revealing to the press that their marriage had descended into a drink- and drug-fuelled nightmare, Michael had secretly 'married' Shaun at a ceremony on the island of Hawaii. The two men had exchanged vows and silver rings then repeated a series of promises in front of a minister who blessed the relationship.

On September 17, 1999, Michael gave an interview on OK!TV that provoked an enormous response. He told presenter Fiona Phillips: 'When the circumstances are right, yes I would adopt a child.' He went on: 'The child would be loved. It would be given all the opportunities it wouldn't normally have had.'

His revelation came after two gay Essex businessmen formally adopted test-tube twins they had fathered in the USA. Michael, by now the host of hit TV show *Kids Say The Funniest Things*, was aware of the furore the two men were causing, but was adamant that he would one day like to be a father too. 'My relationship with Shaun has made such a big difference to my life,' he went on. 'Though obviously such a thing happening late in my life was a bit strange and frightening to start with.'

Michael and Shaun began visiting adoption agencies for preliminary talks. 'Just because society isn't used to the idea of same-sex parenting, doesn't mean a gay couple doesn't have the same fathering instincts as any other couple,' he insisted.

But his next huge headline revealed that Michael still wasn't able to fully control himself. On Boxing Day 1999 a classic *News of the World* exclusive broke under the banner: 'I heard someone turning my door handle at 2 a.m.... and it wasn't the Christmas fairy.'

The report revealed how Michael caused uproar at a Christmas party when he tried to strike it lucky with a 6-foot rugby player. Apparently, he chased Phil Stanyon round a dance floor and later tried to slip into his hotel room after getting hold of a key.

Phil and his partner Sally Clarke had expected a luxury weekend of golf, horse-riding and a smart dinner-dance when they arrived at the Gleneagles Hotel in Perthshire on Friday, December 10, for a company do. Phil, who plays rugby in his spare time and works out at the gym every day, works for a specialist engineering firm that makes equipment for North Sea oil rigs. Michael and Shaun were also at the hotel to film a TV interview.

On the night of Saturday, December 11, Phil escorted Sally to the black-tie dinner party and spotted Michael drinking alone on the other side of the room. It was about 11 p.m. 'I decided to go over and wish him all the best,' said Phil. 'He looked as if he'd had a drink or two. He wasn't smartly dressed for a night out, just wearing a diamond-patterned jumper and dark trousers. I congratulated him on his TV work and also for having the courage to be honest about his sex life. I said it must have been a hard decision but that people respected him for it.

'He asked lots of questions about my job, where I was from and what we were doing at Gleneagles. Then, out of the blue, he asked me what my hotel room number was! I was so surprised, I couldn't make one up, so I told him the truth – 93. He didn't give a reason for the question and when I told my colleagues what had happened they all thought it was very funny.'

From then on, the night turned into a Carry On-style farce.

Phil returned to his friends and they moved to the disco in a special marquee attached to the hotel. Michael followed them in. 'Sally and I were dancing and I could see him twirling around a few yards away,' said Phil. 'Then he appeared right beside us. We moved over to another part of the dance floor. Suddenly there he was again, he'd danced over to be beside me. I didn't want anything embarrassing to happen, so we moved away again. Once more he followed.

'By this time it was about 1 a.m. and people began filing back into the hotel. But when we looked at the exit, there he was, waiting by the only door out. At this stage I was a touch nervous; he'd made his intentions clear on the dance floor. So I grabbed Sally's hand and we dashed out of the marquee through a fire exit at the back.

'It was freezing outside, all snow and rain, but we ran round trying to find the main hotel entrance for about five minutes. But we couldn't find it anywhere and had to return to the marquee exit. Thankfully, by that time Barrymore had disappeared.'

When Phil and thirty-year-old Sally returned to their room, the apprehensive rugby player knew he had to take drastic action. He pulled out his penknife, levered the number 9 from the woodwork and stuck it back upside down.

'Even though all the other doors were numbered in sequence I thought Barrymore might be in such a state that it would confuse him to see the number 63,' he said. 'By this stage I was really bothered.'

The couple undressed for bed, when suddenly there was a knock at the door. It was about 2 a.m. The ruse hadn't worked. The pair looked at each other in amazement and kept quiet. By now they had almost nothing on. 'I was wearing black boxer shorts and Sally was in a white hotel bathrobe,' Phil added, 'but we thought, at least the door's locked.'

Then the handle started to turn and the door inched open. 'I admit I panicked,' said Phil. 'When I heard the door unlock and saw it start to open, it wasn't the Christmas fairy or Santa with a sackload of presents trying to get in. I made a dive for the bathroom, where I hid in the shower. I was convinced it was Barrymore looking for me.'

Sally was livid that her special night at one of Britain's most exclusive hotels had been gate-crashed. 'Who's there? What's going on?' she shouted out and made a grab for the door handle. The door shut abruptly. But nothing was going to stop Sally finding out what was going on. Quickly opening the door herself, she looked out and spotted three men in the corridor. One was a Gleneagles porter in his distinctive green V-neck jumper. The other two were burly characters in suits and ties. 'What the hell is happening?' she demanded. 'Someone just tried to get into our room.'

Sally said later: 'The porter tried to calm things down and asked if there was a problem. I said, "Yes, there certainly is, someone has got hold of a key and tried to come in. That's not right."'

The unwitting porter asked her to go back into her room. 'But I demanded to know what was going on,' she added, 'so he turned to me and said, "It's Mr Michael Barrymore, Miss. There has been a bit of a misunderstanding." Then Barrymore himself emerged from a recess in the corridor to the right of our room. The two men in suits, who I guess were his minders, went to either side of him and escorted him off past our room. He just looked straight ahead and was marched off.'

Only when Michael had been ushered away did Phil venture out of his hiding place in the shower cubicle. Then the couple sat up talking about their brush with a star. 'We were too nervous to sleep,' admitted Phil.

He and Sally decided not to make a formal complaint to the Gleneagles management. 'It was Christmas and we didn't want to cause any bother on a works do, so at the time we just kept quiet,' Phil said. 'But it was quite outrageous. I could have been drunk, naked and asleep on the bed when someone marched in.'

Desperate to bring some stability back to his life and to carve out a lasting relationship with Shaun, Michael kept a low profile for some weeks. And when, in February 2000, the News of the World's Jon Barnsley called him up and asked if he'd fancy a chat, Michael agreed.

It was a period when he was trying to convince himself that his bouts of alcoholism were behind him. 'Those days are over,' he claimed, insisting that he could now drink in moderation. But all around were reminders of his weakness. 'I have two dogs... a Jack Russell called JD after Jack Daniel's and a Bichon Frise called Sprite,' he smiled ruefully. 'The next one will be called Ice and the one after that Tumbler. Sprite is a right nutcase.'

He continued: 'I like a JD as an aperitif, but my favourite drink is Chablis Premier Cru. Trouble is, I'd look a bit daft shouting that out in the park: "Come here, Chablis! Now!"'

Recalling what he regarded as his dark days, and little realising that the worst days were yet to come, he added: 'Other people would visit [rehabs], but I toured them. It was the only time I got a break. Those days are over, though. They were a waste of time and money thrown away.'

Then, returning to a theme that has run through many of his interviews over the years, he went on: 'But I never had anything inside me when I worked, even in the bad times. That was because the only time I felt any comfort was when I was on stage with that microphone in my hand. But off stage I really felt horrible inside. I was allowing anyone and everyone to control me. Anything for a peaceful life. That's what addicts do.'

Later in that interview, Michael also returned to the subject of adoption with Shaun. 'I saw a little lad running around a hotel and I asked the owner if the boy was his,' he recalled. 'He said, "Yeah, he's adopted. He's from Russia." Out there they keep them in institutions until they're sixteen then chuck them out and they invariably end up on drugs or as prostitutes. We could definitely offer a better life than that. So Shaun and I made some inquiries, but it does take a lot of work. We'd like a sister and a brother so they are together. What's wrong if we're two blokes? All they need is loving and taking care of.'

Within days a pregnant woman named Fiona, already a mother of seven, offered to give Michael and Shaun the baby she was expecting. After reading the report in the *News of the World* she declared: 'Michael would make a fantastic dad. You can see on telly how good he is with kids.'

Fiona, thirty-seven, added: 'I'm tired after having seven

children and I'd thought of giving the new baby to a childless couple when it's born. I feel Michael and Shaun would make great parents and I don't see anything wrong with two gays bringing up a baby. As Michael said, the most important thing is love.'

Fiona insisted she wasn't selling the tot but did say that she would want 'expenses', so she and husband Tony, thirty-six, could move away from their home in Greater Manchester. 'We know this could cause an uproar and I don't want to stay where we are in case the other children are picked on at school,' she continued. 'I've never given up any of my children, but there's only so far money will go. I'd like any health bills and legal fees paid.

'I've always liked Michael and think my child would have a much better chance in life with him. I don't want him going into a care home and, as a Catholic, abortion is out of the question.'

She said that Michael would have to be at the maternity clinic so the handover could go without a hitch. 'I will kiss the baby goodbye and that will be it,' she said. 'I wouldn't want any more contact. Knowing the child will have a good upbringing will be enough for me. I can't think of anyone better than Michael Barrymore.'

The adoption never took place, however, and by April 2000, Michael had other matters to occupy himself with. Since that childhood day when he had taken money from his father's pocket and watched a Norman Wisdom film, he had been consumed with a passionate ambition that was now to be realised. He was about to become a comedy actor in a TV series called Bob Martin, based on the subject of a telly host desperate about his image.

'I'd forgotten what nervousness was like,' he said later. 'I was suddenly the new boy and I had to come up with the goods. But I'd only ever acted in a school play. Bob does the game show slightly differently from the way I would have. It's a character, it's not me. Bob is pathetic, he's a misfit, quite shy, no patience. We couldn't be more different.

'The writers asked me about Bob's sexuality but I said I had no hang-ups and they should write it the way they wanted. It's taken me close on forty years to get this part, but I wanted to wait for something good.'

Things were looking good again, but it seemed that Michael was fated to always take two steps forward and one back. In the same month, April 2000, he made a fool of himself yet again at the London Restaurant Awards – and this time his victim was TV's *Wish You Were Here?* presenter Mary Nightingale.

Michael was clearly the worse for wear after swigging from a huge bottle of champagne. Then he spotted 36-year-old Mary in a sheer dress. To the amazement of guests – even those who knew what he could be capable of – he leapt up, grabbed Mary then turned her upside down before collapsing on top of her.

Mary did her best to cover her embarrassment by smiling at a pal: 'I wish he hadn't done that. I wasn't wearing any knickers!' The picture of Mary in a state of disarray made most of the following morning's papers.

But Mary wasn't his only target that night. Earlier in the evening he had pawed a Swiss journalist and wrestled her to the floor. He also ripped a male diner's dress shirt before being led away by Ronan Keating.

And as he presented the prize for best British restaurant, Michael poked fun at the contenders before dismantling the microphones and taking the potted plants and light fittings away with him when he left the stage.

Hours after the ceremony a simmering feud between Michael and comedian Bob Monkhouse erupted into a full-blown war of words. The two men had not been on speaking terms since Michael mocked Monkhouse for using an autocue at the TV Game Show Awards two years earlier.

'Professionally I admire the man immensely – he's a great entertainer,' said Monkhouse through gritted teeth. 'Personally I don't like him. That is to say, I did like him before he became a big star. We got on well. But since then his behaviour towards me has been inexplicably horrible – boorish and insulting.'

Launching his attack in a newspaper review of *Bob Martin*, Monkhouse added: 'Are Barrymore's loyal fans likely to confuse the real-life Barrymore with Bob Martin, the big-headed, foul-mouthed, envious, ungrateful, greedy, self-obsessed, ignorant and petty-minded game show host he portrays so very convincingly and effortlessly? Are Smurfs blue? Is George Best yellow [a cruel reference here to Best's jaundice]?'

The morning after his awards debacle, Michael went back to work on a second series of *Bob Martin*. The first series had been recorded long before transmission.

Bob Mills, co-writer and producer of the show, admitted Michael's bizarre behaviour at the London Restaurant Awards could not have come at a worse time. 'We were trying to get people like Stephen Fry and Alan Bennett to appear in *Bob Martin*,' he said. 'We had our heads in our hands.' But in Michael's defence, he added: 'Any problems that he has, all his problems, come from the fact that he is a decent, slightly naive and open man working in a business where they aren't the best qualities to have.'

The viewing figures for *Bob Martin* must have come as a bit of a shock to the system, though. *My Kind of Music* could pull in 15 million viewers. *Bob Martin* managed 6 million for its first episode. But that went down to 4 million when fans decided that guest stars such as Anthea Turner, Shane Richie and Luke Goss weren't their kind of people.

Still, Michael's performance won rave reviews from his co-stars. Comic actor Keith Allen said: 'I could never envisage the day that I'd be working with Michael Barrymore, so you can imagine my surprise when the script came through the post. Then there were the times I'd go out and people would ask me, "What are you doing next?" And when I'd say, "I'm working with Barrymore", they'd reply, "F*** me, that's your career over, then", because they think I'm working on a game show.

'But to say I'm working with him in drama is something else. People do love him. It was a real pleasure and he is excellent.'

And despite the depressing lack of viewers, Michael made it clear he loved the show. 'They are bloody good scripts,' he said excitedly. 'What's great about it is that the script says a lot of things you'd like to say to people but you never do.'

With a clutch of awards on his mantelpiece and his new acting role, Michael still had one unfulfilled ambition – to work in New York. That dream came true when he filmed a three-part series called *Barrymore on Broadway*. It was screened in July 2000.

'I've dreamed of going to Broadway since I was a kid,' Michael told the press, wearing a wide smile. 'Ever since I saw Norman Wisdom and, later, *The Sound of Music*, I've been totally mesmerised.'

Among the stars Michael encountered were British singer Elaine Paige, who recalled appearing nude in *Hair*. He chatted to Marni Nixon, who provided the vocals for Deborah Kerr in *The King And I* and for Audrey Hepburn in *My Fair Lady*. Then came an unscheduled meeting with a true megastar – he spotted Dane Edna Everage in the street while 'she' was on her way to her Boadway show. As he prepared to leave the Big Apple, Michael confessed: 'I was worried it wouldn't live up to expectations but I've had a fantastic time. I'm enjoying living life. The hardest thing is liking myself and I think I've started to do that.'

Of course, with the future looking calm and settled for once, something was bound to go horribly wrong.

In August 2000, it was revealed that police were investigating allegations of rape against a member of a group of people who had been on a night out with Michael. A vice girl accused a man of forcing her to have sex in a suite, allegedly booked by Michael, at the five-star Berkeley Hotel in London's Belgravia. The man concerned strenuously denied the allegations. Michael was interviewed by police and there was no suggestion he had any knowledge of the alleged offence. But four months later, in December, Michael was cautioned because detectives investigating the case had found Ecstasy, cocaine and cannabis in the hotel room.

Explaining the incident, a friend of his said: 'He was out drinking in London when he met some blokes. The problem he always had was he was too generous for his own good and everyone knew he had money, so they always expected him to put his hand in his pocket first. Of course, it was effectively another audience and Michael was eager to please and he wanted to keep the evening going so he offered to pay for an hotel room so they could keep drinking after the bars closed.

'But around Michael, things have a habit of getting way out of control. Before he knew it, some of the blokes had invited some girls back to the room. Michael only fancied a drink so after a while he felt a bit uncomfortable and left. It was only later, he told me, that after he'd gone one of the women said she'd been raped by one of the blokes. Of course, the police descended on the place and found drugs – and Michael's name was on the room bill.

'Shaun wasn't happy that he'd been in the room at all, and even Michael accepted that it was absolute madness to go there with complete strangers in the first place. But that's Michael in drink for you. Totally barking.'

# 17

# 'I WAS SHAKING LIKE A LEAF AS I CALLED MY MUM'

SHAUN DAVIS wasn't the only important addition to Michael's personal life as the 20th century drew to a close and a new era started. Just before the two men had met, Michael had become reunited with his mother Margaret and his overriding devotion to her would ultimately bring about his break-up with Shaun.

Michael had not spoken to his mother since 1990. To be fair, their relationship had been patchy since the Seventies and the family rows over that failed newsagents and sweetshop in Bermondsey. Bit by bit the bonds that tied mother and son unravelled. And, of course, the fact that Margaret and Cheryl disliked each other didn't help at all. Michael's family dubbed her 'The Rich Bitch'. Cheryl, in turn, called them 'The Family From Hell'.

## A MAN POSSESSED

To understand how Michael and Shaun's relationship could be fractured by a re-kindling of relations with his mum, you have to go back to a day in April 1998. Michael was being driven down the motorway in a Range Rover after filming a TV commercial and was sitting silently in the back of the car. He been like this often, and in the rare moments he'd talked about what was troubling him, he admitted he was thinking about his mum.

His personal assistant Mike Brown knew the signs and reckoned it was high time he helped sort things out. 'Look' he said, passing a mobile phone over the seat to his boss, 'I've got your mum's number keyed into the phone, why don't you ring her now. She's eighty-odd, if anything happens to her you'll never be able to live with it for the rest of your life.'

Michael recalled: 'I took the phone and Maurice Leonard, one of the producers who was in the car with us, told me, "Yes, I think you should do it too." I was more nervous dialling her number than I've been performing in front of the Royal Family. It had been gnawing at me for years. I kept thinking if something terrible happened, how would I deal with it? I sat looking at the number on the screen of the phone for about ten minutes – everything went racing through my mind. She meant the world to me – what if I was rejected? Pressing the "call" button was so hard because I didn't know how she'd react.

'I was shaking like a leaf as I made the call. Then I was talking to my mum but I was a bit taken aback because she didn't know it was me. I'm on telly every week but she'd forgotten my voice. It isn't the same sound on the telephone and she's deaf as a post, God bless her.

'I invited her out for a meal but she said she had the family coming over on Sunday and invited me over there to lunch will all of them. She made me so happy with that invitation, I can't put it in to words. After the phone call, I went very quiet and still. An enormous sense of relief swept over me. Mum still lives in the same three-bedroom flat in the East End that we had when I was a baby.'

'It was strange, going up in the lift for the first time in years. But the minute I stepped through the front door I belonged. In the living room there were old photos of me as a boy – old sepia ones and even shots of me as a baby. It was like I hadn't been away at all. It didn't matter that it had been eight years, which had felt like fifteen – whether it was eight months, eight days or eight hours, I was at home.'

A friend of Michael's took up the story: 'They all sat to together in the front room and Michael told me that his mum never once brought up the subject of the past eight years of silence. "It's incredible," he told me, "She could have had a right go at me and I'd have sat there and taken it." But she didn't, she just smiled at him and held his hand and chatted away as if they'd seen each other a day or so before.'

Michael himself added: 'Seeing Mum smile meant the world to me. I was as complete as I could be – anything on top of this was going to be a bonus.'

When Margaret was interviewed soon after that April meeting, she said: 'At first, when I got the phone call I wasn't quite sure who I was talking to. I thought this voice said "Kieran", which is his real name – a good Gaelic name. And I said, "My Kieran?" and he replied, "Yes", and I said, "Oh my God." I was so excited afterwards – I was crying tears of joy. My first instinct was to phone everybody and tell all my friends. But I held back, because I didn't want anything to go wrong. I was on edge from the Thursday until the Sunday. And on the Sunday he turned up with a huge basket of flowers and chocolates, but most important of all he was home again.'

The visit also reunited Michael with his sister Anne, her husband Colin and their children Mark, twenty-three, and nineteen-year-old Nicola, along with Margaret's great-grandson Liam, whom Michael had never seen.

Margaret said: 'At first we were all a bit lost for words. Michael had missed seeing his nephews and nieces grow up and there were tears – lots of them. We are very emotional as a family. There we all were in the same house where he was born – a family again. It was just so good to be together again.

'When we all sat down it was so natural, as if I'd seen him

only last week. We carried on the family conversation as though he'd been there the previous Sunday. It was just as if he had never been away – his bedroom was still there if he ever needed it.

'The whole family never missed watching Michael's shows and I'd never given up hope that one day we'd be together again. I always enjoyed his programmes on the telly – but I did my crying after they'd finished. I know he had suffered too in those years. There were people I know who even stopped watching him because of what had happened to the family.

'Some friends had said to me, "I suppose your such-and-such son didn't turn up." But on the Monday after his visit I was able to tell them so proudly that he had. Ever since our chat I was been smiling – he made me the happiest mum in the world,' she said happily.

'Our family over in Ireland were thrilled too that he was happy at last. Michael always loved going back over there. As a child he went back every year from the age of two. It doesn't matter what you do in life, if you are not happy then there is no point in it. I always told my children, "Do whatever you want and do it well. If you sweep the roads, then sweep them clean."'

Though she might not have criticised Cheryl at that first meeting, Margaret did later speak out against her former daughter-in-law. 'I desperately wanted her to be part of our family, but it wasn't to be,' she sighed. 'I think Michael stayed away from me because she was jealous, which was silly because whatever love he might have felt for me it was totally different to love he felt for his wife. You don't love your wife less just because you love your mum. It wasn't until Michael parted from his wife that he felt able to get in touch with me.'

Overjoyed that they had finally been reunited, Michael tried to persuade his mum to live in a bungalow next to his mansion in Roydon. But she refused to leave her flat. 'All my memories are there,' she explained. 'All my children grew up there and if I listen hard enough I can still hear their voices when they were babies.'

Michael's great public show of reconciliation with his mum did not come until October 1999, when he took her to the National TV Awards.

His pal explained: 'Margaret might have been eighty-odd and a bit deaf, but otherwise she was a very together woman, very tall like her son and very upright and dignified. She arrived at the Royal Albert Hall on his arm and you could tell she was having the time of her life spotting all the stars that she'd only ever seen on TV, but who stopped and chatted to her and her son like they were old friends. She was in her element.

'Occasionally she'd spot someone she liked – such as Richard Whitely from *Countdown* – and dispatch Michael with the order, "Get him over here and introduce me." Off Michael would obediently go, all smiles, and bring back celeb after celeb to his mother's side. At last there was something from his world that he could give his mother besides money, and he loved every minute of it. It was a magical night for them both.'

Michael won a special lifetime achievement award that night, and wept as he paid an emotional tribute to his mother at the ceremony. He told the star-studded audience: 'I walked back through her door after eight years and it was like I had just walked out of it yesterday.'

The new-found relationship with Margaret buoyed him up – without her the secret excesses that were consuming him would certainly have shattered him sooner. Michael even revealed that his first series of *Bob Martin* had to be cleaned up – because Margaret had complained that the script was too blue. 'One episode featured twenty-seven F-words, well over the guidelines,' he explained. 'She's a strict Irish Catholic who saw the scripts and asked why I had to swear all the time. I explained it wasn't me, it was the character – but we cut down anyway. Now I have an average of two F-words an episode.'

But on March 21, 2001, Michael received a body blow he was in no position to counter – he discovered Margaret had cancer. And although he wasn't to know it at the time, it was also to signal the end of his relationship with Shaun.

'The night he was told about her illness had already been traumatic,' said his pal. 'Michael often infuriates people, but he's never done it on purpose, he hates upsetting anyone. But that night he'd had to settle himself to get rid of two of his production aides. They'd both been with him for ages and he hated having to do it. Inevitably, he was drinking too – the usual, Chablis and then Jack Daniel's. Shaun hated it when he got this way, he really did care for Michael and would go mad with frustration when he saw the damage Michael was doing to himself. Desperately, Shaun was trying to think of something that would take Michael's mind off his next drink. He knew that Margaret would want to talk to her son about her illness, if only to tell him not to worry about her. Time and again Shaun repeated, "Michael, you really must phone your mum, this is serious. She has cancer." But Michael didn't know how to cope with his grief and nor did he want to communicate that to his mum, he didn't want to risk breaking down over the phone. "I'll call her later," he kept saying.

'Shaun pushed it and pushed it and eventually Michael snapped and started throwing things around the kitchen. There was crockery and smashed glass everywhere.

'That did it for Shaun, he couldn't cope with the drinking and the wildness and the drug-taking any more. He got up from the table, marched into the bedroom, packed a bag and walked out of Michael's life. Michael was devastated.'

But Michael was rarely lost for male company. And waiting in the wings was a man he had already met: John Kenney.

# 18

# COUNTDOWN
# TO HORROR

MICHAEL HAD met John at the gay bar Bromptons in London's Earls Court, in early February 2001. He could not have known then that together they would live through the greatest disaster of his life – the death of Stuart Lubbock.

John, who had been brought up on a rundown Newcastle estate where you kept any gay thoughts strictly to yourself, had fathered three children in his teens. But eventually he could not deny the urges that were within him, urges he was never likely to reconcile in his home area, before he came out of the closet. So he packed his bags and headed south and west across the country to the bright lights of Blackpool. Here he would encounter few problems about his sexuality. There was such a fluid population in Blackpool, drawn in by the piers, the shows, the sands and the astonishing Pleasure Beach centre, that he could easily lose himself. He was also drawn to glitter and the fringes of showbiz and before long he found work dressing as a drag queen called Miss Racquel in a revue bar called Funnygirls.

Funnygirls, just back from the sea front, is one of the most popular nightspots in Blackpool. The drag queens there dress with more glamour than Marilyn Monroe on a night out and strut their stuff on either a stage or the bar tops as the fancy takes them. The place can be heaving – and Miss Racquel, the striking figure in lurex, big blonde wig and bright red lipstick that shimmered under the lights, was a star.

'I'm normally a quiet, softly spoken man,' said John with a smile. 'But when I become Miss Racquel I'm a totally outrageous person and they love me.' Working in a drag bar, John was well used to over-the-top behaviour, but even he was shocked by the way Michael conducted himself.

Recalling that first night after he had nipped south from Blackpool for a break in London, John said: 'I saw him and did a double-take. I knew who he was from the telly, of course. I used to look at him on TV and think he was quite sexy. I like the mature look with greying hair and he had nice big brown eyes. That night he was wearing beige jeans and top with a chocolate brown jacket, but he looked much older in the flesh.'

The pair chatted... well, as much as they could because, as

ever, Michael was hugely in demand with people coming up to say hello and bathe in his limelight for precious moments. By now he also had a widespread reputation within the gay community for picking up strangers, so there was always the possibility that one of them might 'strike it lucky'. But that night Michael had eyes only for John, even though John had arrived with his flatmate, a man called Gerry.

'He said he liked me because I looked straight, not gay,' John said, recalling the conversation that was to change the path of his life for ever. 'He tried to kiss me in the club and I pushed him away because everyone was watching. Michael couldn't understand it. He said, "What are you doing? Give me a kiss." I said. "No" and told him it was because we were in a nightclub and him being who he is.'

Michael had arrived at the club with another friend, but that man had wanted to go home early. Michael, feeling suddenly vulnerable among strangers, turned to John and said, 'You'll look after me, won't you?'

Even though he was with Gerry, John replied that he would. What else could he say? 'I didn't think much of it at the time,' he said. 'It was just the sort of thing you say to be polite.'

It was about 2.15 a.m. when they emerged from the nightclub on to a cold London street. Now that they were away from other clubbers, John thought that was the end of it, especially as he felt he had offended Michael by not giving in to that kiss. He didn't feel that Michael would want looking after any more.

'We came out of the club and I said: "Oh well, it was nice to meet you,' revealed John. But Michael wasn't giving up that easily, he turned to me on the pavement and said, "I thought you were looking after me."

'I told him, "Yes I did. and I have looked after you. And now it's time to go home." He asked where I lived and I told him that Gerry and I shared a flat in Hammersmith.'

Michael asked: 'Can I come back with you?'

John was immediately struck by how plaintive and alone this huge star sounded. He could afford virtually anything he fancied, yet all he wanted was to return with a relative stranger to a flat in West London.

'I said, "Yeah – you can come back for a cuddle if you like,' recalled John. Michael was a bit jet-lagged because he'd just flown back from a holiday in Hawaii. In the taxi with Gerry and me, Michael tried to kiss me again, but I refused.'

Back at the flat, John dashed into the kitchen and got out the best glasses. Thank God they had some wine in. Michael, though, made himself completely at home and asked how old John was.

'Michael thought I was twenty-six,' he said. 'I told him I was twenty-nine, even though I was thirty then. I put on some music. But Michael was falling asleep on the sofa, so I told him to get his head down.'

Clearly though, Michael wasn't about to fall asleep just then.

'He followed me into my bedroom and we both stripped down to our boxers,' John recalled. 'He always wore white Boss ones. Michael was getting a bit saucy and I warned him he was only back for a cuddle, but he ignored me and took off his boxers. I drifted off but then woke up at 4.30 a.m. to hear him snoring and told him it was time to go. He wasn't pleased.'

The pair moved to the lounge so Michael could use John's mobile to call a cab. It was then that he admitted he was still seeing Shaun Davis. John was disappointed, but adamant. 'I wasn't interested if he wasn't single,' he said firmly. 'I told him to leave and he said, "Well, everyone knows I've got a boyfriend."'

Apparently, everyone didn't know.

'It was the first I'd heard of it,' confessed John. 'He kissed me goodbye on the cheek and as he was walking out the door he said, "I don't think you could handle it, this lifestyle." I said to him, "What makes you think you can handle mine?" I didn't care that he was a TV star, I simply didn't want to get involved with someone who had a boyfriend.'

Little did John know just what a lifestyle he was getting into. And despite his protestations that he didn't want to get involved, it was just ten days after that first, fateful meeting at Bromptons that he found himself marvelling at the trapping of seemingly limitless wealth at Michael's Roydon mansion.

'After Michael had left my flat I saw he'd left his jacket and packet of Silk Cut cigarettes,' he explained. 'He'd given me his phone number that first night, so I dialled it on my mobile and got through to Brownie (Michael Brown) his PA. A girl called Chrissie came to pick up his stuff a week later.

'The day after she'd been to see me, Brownie rang and said, "Michael would like you to join him for dinner." When I asked about Shaun, Brownie said, "No he's gone. He's finished with him."'

John could not have guessed at the traumas that had precipitated Shaun's leaving. But now it was his turn to get the star treatment as Michael turned on the charm. 'Michael sent a car over for me, a silver Mercedes 280E with his driver,' said John, who felt like a million dollars as he sat behind the smoked glass, and luxuriated in the upholstery. So this is how the other half lives, he thought. Then, as a flash of reality burst through the reverie, he found himself wondering, what the hell am I doing here? I don't even know this man.

Michael was at the mansion to greet him with open arms. The fridge was full of drink and, in the lounge, John could feel his feet sink into the deep pile carpet.

It wasn't long before Michael asked his new guest to share in his excesses. John recalled: 'I'd been there about an hour and a half when Michael turned to me in the kitchen and said, "Do you fancy a line of coke?" It was as though he were offering me a cup of tea. He got the stuff out of his pocket and it was in a wrap of paper. He tipped some out on to the granite worktop, chopped it up with a credit card and then snorted it through a rolled-up £20 note.

'Michael told me the first time he'd had coke someone had given it to him when he was really tired. He thought it didn't do anything. Then he realised he was wide awake. But it didn't have that affect on him any more. He told me he liked it now because it improved his sex drive. It certainly did make him feel chatty and frisky.'

John was no stranger to cocaine – he used it on weekends and, compared to Michael, considered himself to be more of a 'recreational' user. So that day, in the mansion kitchen at Roydon, faced with an offer of illegal drugs from a household favourite star, he thought, why not?

He confessed: 'I had a line and it gave me the usual buzz. The cocaine also seemed to make Michael a little perkier. Then we moved to the lounge and listened to his favourite CDs – The Carpenters, Roberta Flack and The Fugees. It's ironic now that "our song" became "Killing Me Softly". Michael liked to sing along, but he's got a rubbish voice.'

As they wandered from room to room, John was able to get a feeling for his host's taste. 'Michael's house is very tastefully done, lots of 1930s art deco stuff,' he said. 'But he has an obsession with straightening things. His housemaid Maria puts everything on the diagonal, things like a box on a coffee table.

It drove him mad so after she left he'd go round the house squaring everything up.'

That night, after the coke, out came the Jack Daniel's, one of Michael's favourite tipples. 'After a few JD and Sprites I was far more relaxed,' John added. It was then that Michael made his move.

'We sat on his Gucci sofa and he put his arms around me and started kissing me passionately,' said John. 'He gets aroused very quickly and he said to me, "Do you want to go to bed?" I said "Yes."'

Michael led John to the master bedroom – the same one he once shared with Cheryl, and then with Shaun. 'It's painted magnolia with an en suite bathroom and lots of wardrobes and units,' revealed John. 'The bed has a huge leather headboard and there's a vast mirror on the wall at the end of the room with light bulbs around it – like one you'd find in a studio dressing room. When you're on the bed you can see yourself in the mirror. I remember that the bed was made up with pure white crisp cotton sheets.'

Though the cocaine had made Michael perkier, it had the opposite effect on John. 'Michael started kissing me passionately on the bed, but I wasn't aroused because I'd done coke,' he said. 'To be honest, it was all going a bit fast for me, because it was only the second night I'd known him. I asked him if he had any condoms and he said he never used them.'

Coke or not, John wasn't so far gone that he didn't think about precautions. 'I said, "No condoms, no sex," he explained. "So we had oral sex instead, and that seemed to satisfy him. Afterwards we fell asleep in each other's arms."'

But despite Michael's protestations, John was worried that he was actually still seeing Shaun Davis. 'There were pictures of him and Shaun all over the house,' he said. 'It was him and Shaun arm in arm. They were on the wall in the hallway, in the lounge and one next to the bed. I turned that one face down, I didn't want to look at it. That became a routine for me, but Michael didn't notice.'

Well, not until many days later.

'I remember that one day Michael phoned me,' said John. 'He must have looked at the bedside table and twigged. He said, "Do you keep putting them face down? Sorry, I should have realised." The next time I went there, the photos had vanished.'

It wasn't the only thing that vanished. John had noticed that on their first night together in Bromptons, Michael had been wearing a thick platinum ring. Three weeks later, that was gone too.

'When I asked where the ring had gone, he said he didn't need it any more because Shaun gave it to him when they got married,' John revealed. 'I said to him, "Two men can't get married. What are you doing stupid things like that for?" Michael got very defensive and snapped: "What do you mean?"

I said, "I don't agree with it. That sort of marriage is not recognised in the eyes of the law."

'He just shrugged his shoulders.'

But this was a relatively minor argument in a relationship that, like so many before in Michael's life, appeared to be going from strength to strength. Though they were worlds apart, both men had come from tough working-class backgrounds and shared the bond of struggling to come to terms with their true sexuality.

'Despite everything, Michael seemed desperately lonely,' John reflected, with a sigh. 'I had an urge to look after him because he had had a terrible battle to admit he is gay. He came out late in life. I'd been through all that turmoil from the ages of thirteen to seventeen. I tried to overdose when I was sixteen because I couldn't handle being a dad, yet also having sexual feelings towards men. I had two girlfriends pregnant at the same time and I was trying to prove [that I was] something I wasn't.

'I told my mum, but she couldn't comprehend it. I said, "I've got something to tell you, Mum", and she said, "What's that?"

'I said, "I'm gay", and she said, "I'm very happy as well." When I explained that I was homosexual, she replied. "You've got children. How can you be gay?" But I persisted and told her I had feelings for men. She was totally shocked.'

It was John's turn to be shocked when, one night as they

lounged in the mansion, Michael hatched a plan to hire a male prostitute that they could both share. It was another example of his continuing compulsion to put himself in dangerous situations with complete strangers.

John revealed: 'We were sitting on the sofa fooling around when he suddenly suggested, "Should we ring a rent boy?" I said no straight away. I thought it was a disgusting idea and it made me feel cheap. Michael's face changed and he insisted, "I was only joking."'

'But there was another night when we had an argument because he wanted to phone a gay chatline. I kicked up a fuss because I found it degrading and asked him, "Why do you want to use a chatline when I'm here?" He said he was curious because he'd never done it before.

'He got out of bed and I followed him to the lounge, where I saw him on the portable phone. I asked what he was doing and he said, "Oh nothing" and hung up.'

John already knew that Michael wasn't shy about telling him what he wanted in bed – or out of it. 'He loved to talk dirty and he was always directing me when we had sex,' he said. 'He was quite graphic in his descriptions.'

Small bottles of amyl nitrate or poppers were also tucked away in a bedside drawer. 'We both sniffed it during sex,' John confessed. 'It's a very overpowering liquid which makes you euphoric because your blood pressure goes through the roof. It really turned him on but it gave me a terrible headache the next day.'

John also revealed that during their sex games, Michael would also invent a new persona for himself, as if he couldn't bear to be the same person when he was giving himself up to his excessive urges as the one his fans loved on stage. 'He called himself Mr Dobbs,' said John. 'One night I was in the bedroom and he came in from the bathroom holding his Oral B toothpick and announcing in a creepy voice, "Hello little boy. I'm Mr Dobbs." I fell in with the play-acting and said, "Oh Mr Dobbs. Where are you from?" and he said, "Dobbs Weir", which is a village near his home in Essex.

'Mr Dobbs then tried to bite me on the neck. Every now and then he would make an appearance. I used to think he was going to mentally torture me with Mr Dobbs. He was quite scary.'

An excited Michael once led John outside to the garden and pool areas, where he said he had 'a surprise' waiting. On the external brick wall of the lounge, Michael had painted in pale blue foot-high letters: Mr Dobbs Was 'Ere.

'I was absolutely stunned,' said John. 'The house was immaculate, but he actually daubed graffiti on his own place! It was an incredible thing to do. The moment I saw it I told Michael he was a nutter and crazy. He just laughed hysterically... But I also remember another occasion when I got a phone call and someone else was in the room and took the call. She said, "Excuse me John, but it's for you, there's a Mr Dobbs on the phone and he sounds like a right creep."'

A little over three weeks into their relationship, Michael took John to the five-star Chewton Glenn country house hotel in New Milton, Hampshire. If Kenney had been bowled over by Michael's Mercedes and then his mansion, this was in a different league entirely. The hotel boasts a Michelin-starred French restaurant and an enormous croquet lawn.

John got a true taste of Michael's party mood on the way down there. He explained: 'Brownie got me put on Michael's car insurance so I could drive us to Chewton Glen. This time it was in a different Mercedes, a silver Mercedes 500 S Class.

'It was a Saturday, so I took the car during the day and picked Michael up from home at 5.30 p.m. He immediately sat in the passenger seat and opened a bottle of wine. I thought it was a bit early for a drink, but I didn't say anything. Then he popped a Valium and when I asked what it was for, he told me, "I get panic attacks."

'Once we got to Chewton Glen, we proceeded to get very drunk. We had a couple of lines of coke before dinner and by the time my meal arrived, I'd lost my appetite.

'Michael, meanwhile, was fascinated by this Italian waiter called Guido and across the room he yelled a particularly crude remark. Roughly translated it meant, "Are you gay?" I was so embarrassed. Later that evening we met two girls and their husbands and I couldn't believe it when Michael invited them all up to our suite. He got out the coke and did it in front of them.

'The next day I said to him, "You can't afford to do that. They could have been anyone." But he wasn't worried in the least.'

Yet again, Michael was pushing his luck to the limit with complete strangers. But with acquaintances, he could be even more outrageous, especially when he took it into his mind to play host and cook. Michael's party piece, John confided, was a traditional roast dinner – with a secret ingredient. With a glass of wine by his side, Michael would load the baking tray with a plump leg of lamb with potatoes, carrots and parsnips around the sides. Then there'd be a grind of salt and pepper on top. So far so good, everything appeared normal.

When the succulent joint was roasted to perfection, Michael would remove the meat and veg and leave the juices bubbling in the pan as he spooned in some flour and water to make gravy. Except that adding an Oxo cube for flavour wasn't part of the recipe. Instead, he held a cheese grater over the dish and discreetly shred marijuana hash into the sauce.

And while the drug took hold on unsuspecting guests, said John, Michael would sit and grin like the Cheshire cat. 'It became a standing joke between us,' he said. 'If you go to Michael's for a meal, don't have the gravy.'

John first discovered the added ingredient when Michael played host to a seventy-year-old neighbour called Jean. He explained: 'Michael cooked lamb with all the trimmings. He carved the meat and told Jean, "Oh put loads of gravy on John's plate." All through the meal he kept asking me what I thought of the gravy. Later, when Jean had left, I said, "OK, what did you do to the gravy?" He told me he'd put hash in it. After that I'd often see him grating the hash, which looked like a hunk of chocolate, with a cheese grater. It happened whenever we had guests over for a roast. It certainly used to do the trick. We'd be laughing till our sides ached.

'One night Michael invited his pal Geoff Pope, the TV writer, and his wife Tina over. He poured loads of gravy on Geoff and Tina's plates and sat back with a straight face while they tucked in. They had no idea what was going on and started getting a bit giggly.

'We'd been drinking before the meal so they probably thought they were just getting drunk very quickly. I know that's how I felt when I first had the gravy. Between mouthfuls, Geoff kept saying, "This is delicious, Michael." He suspected nothing. Michael was looking at me and winking as Geoff got more and more woozy.

'Then Michael got a fit of giggles and had to leave the table. By this stage everyone else was giggling as well, because we were all stoned.'

For John's 31st birthday, Michael booked a three-day weekend at Ireland's Ashford Castle, a luxury hotel overlooking Lough Corrib near Galway. Previous VIP guests included Prime Minister Tony Blair and Hollywood hero John Wayne. But the refined traditions of clay pigeon shooting and golf were the last thing on Michael's mind.

'We flew there the night after Geoff Pope had been over for dinner,' explained John. 'No sooner had we arrived than we hired a rowing boat and went out fishing for salmon and trout on the lake. But even though Michael is a keen fisherman, he soon got bored with that.

'So we came back to shore and handed back the rods and wandered back to the castle. But on our way there, Michael stopped me and said excitedly, "Look at them bushes over there." I could see he was pointing to a row of beautifully manicured trees near the stables.

'He said urgently, "Come on, we'll go in there" and when I asked why, he added, "Oh just to have a look." But the scenery turned out to be the last thing on Michael's mind. Amid the branches, Michael slumped into the dirt, unzipped John's trousers and began to perform a sex act on him.

John was nonplussed. He recalled: 'I told him, "Hang on, there's people walking past" and I pulled away from him. He told me to come back but I refused. Michael really did get off on the risk element. But I could just imagine the fuss if we got caught. How would we explain our way out of that one? Other guests had already recognised him at the castle.'

That night they were looking forward to a special meal in the castle's sensational restaurant. Just one problem: their luggage had got lost on the way over and all they had were the clothes they stood up in – and the knees of Michael's trousers were already a bit the worse for wear.

'Michael was insistent that we needed something smart for dinner so he rang down to the Castle boutique and asked for a range of clothes for us to choose from. He bought me a shirt and tie, a navy cashmere blazer and some grey cords. As I stood there in my new threads, he smiled and said, "You look quite sexy, just like Will Carling."

'He then bought a dark brown cashmere jacket, some beige trousers, a white shirt and the same tie as me, which had the Ashford Castle logo on it. His jacket was a bit short though, because he's so tall. In all I think the bill for clothes came to about £1,500.'

When they arrived back home, Michael's by now familiar tendency to indulge himself to excess came once more to the fore. 'If ever there was a bit of coke powder left over, he'd dab it with his finger and rub it on his gums,' John disclosed. 'And if that didn't work, he'd pop a Valium instead. He'd carry a strip of the pills in his pocket.

'If he had nothing planned, Michael would start drinking at

about 3 p.m. He'd start on the white wine, like Chablis and Chardonnay. And by the time I'd get to see him, around 7.30 p.m., he was already well on his way.'

John would watch dumbfounded at Michael's thirst for booze. He regularly downed a bottle of wine in twenty minutes. And when he wasn't on the wine, Michael would revert to his favourite tipple of Jack Daniel's and Sprite.

'He keeps crates of Sprite and Coca-Cola in his laundry room,' John revealed. 'And in the kitchen cupboard next to the fridge freezer he usually had five or six unopened bottles of JD. He could easily get through half of one of those 750ml bottles, which he'd mix up with cans of Sprite.'

At this stage of his interview, John sighed. 'Michael has a lot of personal demons,' he admitted, 'and if he can't run away, he wants to block it out with booze and drugs. He used to say to me, "All I ever wanted was a sandwich shop. I never asked for all this." I truly believe he's on a self-destruct mission.'

John saw evidence for that even more clearly when Michael took him on a three-day trip to Amsterdam in March, 2001. Two nights before, Michael had humiliated himself by abusing the audience at a charity function he was hosting for the Make A Wish Foundation at London's Park Lane Hilton. The 1,300-strong audience, including Virgin boss Richard Branson, sat aghast as the comic made crude and abusive jokes about sex and drugs.

'As you can see, I'm still in rehab,' Michael told the assembled guests. 'I've got a joint full of dope and an expensive suite upstairs. If anyone wants to join me later for sex, they're welcome.'

John shuddered at the thought of the evening. 'I was supposed to go but in the end I was too tired,' he explained. 'Michael later told me he'd lost his rag because they were all talking over him when he wanted to speak. I said to him in exasperation, "Look what happens when I leave you for a night." And he said, "Well, you shouldn't have left me."'

The trip to Amsterdam was hastily organised to get Michael out of the spotlight, but as soon as they checked into their room Michael and John went to a cafe to buy a bag of strong 'orange bud' dope. 'I bought two slices of space cake – Madeira cake baked with marijuana,' John recalled, 'and he scoffed that. We rolled some joints and we were both totally out of it.

'We were in a cafe called Smokey's Bar and as he drank lager, Michael was dragging on a joint. There were a bunch of English lads in there, they could see he was smoking drugs but again he was too out of his head to notice or to care. Later, back at the hotel, Michael ordered a huge four-course meal because the dope gave him a huge appetite.'

When they returned to the UK, life continued as normal – or what passed for normal in the Barrymore household. But one night, Michael told John of his contempt for the two lovers who had once been the centre of his life – his wife Cheryl and his 'husband' Shaun.

John revealed: 'Michael referred to Cheryl as "the red-haired witch". And he said, "She's dead as far as I'm concerned." There was no love lost there. He also told me how much of a control freak she was.'

Michael also harped on about how desperate he was for children and, said John, blamed Cheryl for ruining his chance to be a dad. It was a grossly unfair accusation to make. 'The fact that he will never father a child of his own really gnaws away at Michael,' John admitted. 'He's fantastic with children. I saw him with friends' kids and they absolutely adored him. I asked him why he never had kids with Cheryl and he said she didn't want them. I didn't ask why. I just left it at that.'

John did not realise that Cheryl had been severely hurt in a car accident years before. But he did tell Michael that he thought it was wrong for two men to bring up a baby as the star had planned to do with Shaun Davis.

'I asked him if it was true that he had planned to adopt a child with Shaun,' he said sombrely. 'He said "Yes", but added that it was Shaun's idea. I told him I didn't agree with it because I believe a child needs a woman as well as a man to bring it up. A marriage with two men just doesn't provide that contrast with a male and a female influence.

'Michael later told to me he never really loved Shaun. The

only person Michael seems to have ever loved is himself.'

Despite their differences, however, the pair seemed to be getting on well. In only a few short days, though, the two of them would be engulfed in tragedy.

# 19

# OF ALL THE CLINICS IN ALL THE WORLD, IT HAS TO BE GAZZA'S!

THE POLICE investigation into Stuart Lubbock's death had given rise to a number of horrific reports. One of them was that he had had 'violent gay sex' with at least one man before he drowned. Stuart had apparently suffered sexual injuries so severe that experts reportedly suspected they had been inflicted with an implement. It also emerged that Michael's neighbours had heard 'hysterical and high-pitched' screams early on the morning of March 31.

The reports, and the speculation about Stuart's sexuality, were devastating to his close family. His mother, Dorothy Hand, grandmother to Stuart's five-year-old daughter and baby son, said bitterly: 'My son's reputation has been destroyed by this. He has always had a girlfriend. All this talk of him being bisexual is rubbish.' Dorothy, sixty, stressed: 'I'd like to put on record, for Stuart's sake, that he was not gay or bisexual. He was completely straight.'

A post mortem examination confirmed that Stuart had drowned. Toxicology and forensic tests revealed he did take drugs shortly before his death. Meanwhile, Stuart's former wife, 27-year-old Susan Homan, said she was stunned at the manner of his death. 'He simply wasn't a party animal,' she stated. 'He never took drugs and didn't drink excessively. There was never any hint that he might be gay or bisexual, far from it.'

Stuart, it emerged, had recently parted from girlfriend Claire Wicks, mother of his children.

On June 1 the police investigation into that terrible night began to take shape in public. John Kenney was warned in advance by his lawyer that he and Michael faced arrest. Stunned by the development, John announced: 'My lawyer David Corker, who also represents Michael, told me police toxicology results have finally come back. These have shown the presence of a controlled drug in Stuart's bloodstream.

'He also said that the drugs were taken shortly before Stuart met his death and definitely while he was at that party. Police have told him that the results are a "matter of concern" and they are now treating me and Michael as suspects. They say that they are not satisfied that I have told them the full picture... I've told the police everything I know but I can't say what happened during the party at Michael's house before I arrived.

'My lawyer said the police don't want to swoop on me in a dawn raid and have asked me to make myself available with Michael at a police station next week. My lawyer has suggested I should go to Michael's house and we'll be arrested together there. But I haven't been able to contact Michael since the lawyer broke the news to me.'

The reason he'd been unable to make contact was because Michael had flown to Dubai, where he was lying low at the luxurious Pyramids leisure hotel complex. But Michael's idea of lying low is significantly different to other people's. Astonished guests saw him downing lager after lager as he went out on town with a male pal.

Later, he joined airline staff for an all-night rooftop pool party where he drank himself unconscious – but not before he had tried to chat up a 24-year-old British tourist in a Dubai club.

Daniel Simpson, who is not gay, said: 'I couldn't believe my eyes when I saw Michael in the club. He was sitting in the corner with another guy at a table littered with cans of Heineken. The two men weren't talking to each other and Michael looked absolutely devastated.

'My pals and I had managed to get into the VIP section on the second floor and Michael tried to come up as well. He was stopped by a bouncer who didn't recognise him and had to say, "Do you know who I am!" before they let him in.

'Anyway, I was standing by the bar with a mate when Michael started staring at me. It made me feel really uncomfortable. Then he walked over, stood very close and asked, "Can I buy you a drink?" I said, "No thanks." To be truthful, he gave me the creeps. He was really tipsy and couldn't stand up properly. He looked a complete wreck.'

Michael, wearing a red and white striped polo shirt and khaki trousers, then walked off and sat with a group of airline cabin crew that Daniel had befriended during his week-long stay. 'Michael wouldn't talk about himself,' he said. 'He just asked about everyone else. He didn't say anything about what was going on back in Britain.'

As the night wore on, Michael discovered that the group were sharing an apartment nearby – and insisted on returning there with them. Though he seemed to have a male companion he was clearly desperate for company, the more the better. At the apartment he continued to down more and more lager before collapsing on a sun lounger in the early hours.

'Towards the end of the party I'd gone to bed and Michael was practically unconscious,' said Londoner Daniel. 'The next morning the friend he was with had to lift him up and help him down to a taxi. I just couldn't believe it was him. After all that had happened you'd think he would want to keep a low profile.'

The eyes of the nation were upon him as Michael flew back to Britain to face arrest. Looking suntanned but grim-faced, he hid behind dark glasses at Heathrow airport and refused to answer questions about the police probe as he walked to a chauffeur-driven silver Mercedes. The following morning, on June 6, he was arrested on drugs allegations as the police announced their investigation into Stuart Lubbock's death was being treated as a murder inquiry.

Though John Kenney had said that they would be arrested at the mansion, plans had changed somewhat and both men made their way separately to Harlow police station. Michael arrived at 8.22 a.m. in an unmarked police car. Dressed in a dark jacket, he was accompanied by his solicitor David Corker and two detectives.

Essex Police later issued a statement confirming that its major investigation team, led by Detective Superintendent Ian McNeill, had made three arrests: 'One man, aged thirty-one, from Blackpool, and one man, aged twenty-six, from Harlow, have been arrested on suspicion of murder,' the terse statement read. 'The third man, aged forty-nine from Roydon, has been arrested on suspicion of possession and supply of a class B drug, possession of a class A drug and allowing premises to be used for the taking of a class B drug.

'Mr Lubbock was found unconscious in the swimming pool of an address in Beaumont Park Drive, Roydon, early on Saturday, March 31, and was declared dead at Princess Alexandra Hospital, Harlow, later that morning. A post mortem examination showed the cause of death to be immersion. Further toxicology tests were conducted, the results of which have been assessed.'

If charged and convicted of the drugs allegations, Michael faced a maximum prison sentence of fourteen years. John and 26-year-old Justin Merritt faced a possible life sentence if they were ultimately to be found guilty of murder. They were devastated beyond belief.

John insisted he was innocent and stressed: 'I did not have sex with Stuart and I don't know who did. What I do know is I did everything I possibly could to save that man's life.'

John's sister Denise, also shocked, added: 'He told me he was going to the police station to answer some questions about the drowning and said he'd be out after an hour. But when I rang the police they told me he was in very serious trouble and, as I was family, I should get down to Harlow in Essex immediately. I was absolutely amazed when I learned he had been arrested on suspicion of murder. It doesn't make any sense. If my brother was involved in a murder, why did he try to save that man's life?'

It had already been an even longer day for Justin Merritt. At 5.45 a.m. that morning, police had buzzed his doorbell. When he opened the door he was arrested. 'I was half asleep when I went to the door and when I saw the detectives I was expecting them to tell me how Stuart had died,' he said. 'Instead they arrested me. When I asked what for, they told me it was on suspicion of murdering Stuart. I couldn't believe it. I couldn't think properly.'

The arrests were the culmination of a police investigation involving eighteen officers. After spending more than twelve hours in custody, all three men were released without charge on police bail pending further inquiries. They were scheduled to reappear at the station on August 15.

Justin expressed his fears that he would be forced to take the blame for the tragedy. 'I'm going to be made a scapegoat, aren't I?' he said. 'But I won't take the blame for others. Whatever happens I feel really sorry that someone died. At the end of the day he was someone's son, someone's dad. It's really sad.'

Michael was given leave to travel abroad to help ease his 'mental turmoil' over the case. He promptly flew to America. But as he jetted out, his brother John Parker launched another stinging attack on his estranged sibling. 'I think it's immoral having these gay sex parties where people are taking drugs,' John commented. 'I was shocked to hear about it.'

No sooner had he landed in the States than Michael took to his usual refuge when the going got tough – he booked into a clinic. This time it was the £4,000-a-week Meadows Clinic in Arizona, where he would receive counselling for his depression and emotional problems. Bizarrely, he checked in for an intensive course of therapy at the same time that soccer idol Paul Gascoigne was being treated there for drink and tranquilliser addictions. It was never made clear if the pair met inside the clinic, though the collision of two such astonishing personalities would have been a sell-out in any theatre in the land.

Gazza had checked in on June 1 after Everton team manager Walter Smith demanded he clean up his act or lose his £20,000-a-week position with the club.

A pal who knows both men, said: 'I wouldn't like to have been another poor patient listening in on those two talking. If you weren't barking when you went in, five minutes with those two would send you right round the bend. Of all the clinics in all the world, how the two of them came to end up in the same place is incredible.'

Most patients stay at the Meadows for at least a month, cut off from family and friends, while they undergo a detoxification and psychological programme. The clinic is a privately owned centre in the foothills of the Great South-West Desert in Tuscon. Over the past year it had gained a reputation as the new hangout for troubled celebrities. Tara Palmer Tomkinson, Daniella Westbrook and Tom Parker Bowles are all former patients.

On July 24, Michael got some good news for a change. The Crown Prosecution Service recommended that he should be charged only with possession of cannabis and allowing it to be used in his home. Compared to his original arrest sheet, this was a comparative slap on the wrist. On August 13 he jetted back into Britain to answer bail. This time he looked fit and well as he touched down at Heathrow, wearing a crumpled beige jacket, a white sports shirt and brown casual trousers.

He managed a brief smile, then strode down the airport corridors. Asked if he had benefited from his clinic stay, he said: 'I'm feeling a lot better, thank you.' Later that day he was safely behind the walls of his Roydon mansion once more. But while it provided security from unwanted questions, the pool was there to jog memories of the awful events of March 31.

Still, he received support from the quarter that mattered most to him. ITV supremo David Liddiment gave Michael his backing and said: 'He's an extraordinarily talented man who's had great difficulties. I see no reason to abandon him.' Michael was delighted. As he never tired of telling anyone, he only felt truly alive in front of an audience. Now, after the worst few months of his life, that audience wasn't being taken away from him. He still had a way back.

But there were still hurdles to be crossed. On August 15, five months after Stuart's tragic death, Essex Police announced that as a result of 'new information', magistrates had granted a warrant to allow them to re-search Michael's home. They were to carry out forensic examinations that would be concentrating on 'specific areas' of the house and its rambling grounds. The operation coincided with press speculation that police now suspected Stuart might have been dead before he fell into the swimming pool. There was now some doubt about whether he would have taken a swim after sustaining those reported sexual injuries.

Shaken to the core, Michael remained at his home while police searched the place from top to bottom. As a convoy of vehicles carrying police and scientists arrived at the property, Michael's lawyer David Corker said: 'He's coping with this, as well as can be expected, but it's an unpleasant intrusion into his privacy and dignity, especially as it's happening for a second time.'

He added: 'Mr Barrymore is shocked and upset… but is co-operating fully with police.' But Mr Corker also stressed that no murder charges had been even remotely associated with his client: 'He has not been questioned about homicide. The police are not here to question him about homicide. There's not been any attempt to question him about homicide. His staff are not being questioned about homicide… The sole reason for today's events is that Mr Barrymore is the occupier of the house in which the death of Mr Lubbock occurred.

'Mr Barrymore wants the police inquiry to be conducted as speedily as possible. That's why there's no inhibition. Mr Barrymore will remain on the premises.'

Following another visit to a police station in Harlow, Michael's bail was extended to October. The same bail extension was granted to John Kenney and Justin Merritt. The relatives of the deceased still knew frustratingly little about the circumstances of his death, and were trusting in the police to shed some light on the mysterious events. Stuart Lubbock's father Terry said: 'I just want to let the police investigation take its course. I have every faith in the British justice system.' His mother Dorothy added: 'We're just leaving everything to the police. I'm as much in the dark as anyone.'

Soon Michael needed another holiday. This time, though, he forsook Dubai and Arizona for the more sedate Norfolk Broads. Holidaymakers were delighted. Tainted by scandal he might be, but he was still one of their favourite stars. Fans watched in amazement as he hired a 42-foot cruiser called *Ultimate Gem 2* for himself and his guests – a young family and a Labrador dog. Michael stocked up with supplies from a store at Kingfisher Quay in Stalham Staithe, near North Walsham, on August Bank Holiday Monday afternoon. The party set sail about an hour later. Michael fed the swans – only for one of them to give him a nasty nip.

Swans apart, this was only a brief interlude of happiness before the next tragedy to blight Michael's life. Less than three weeks later, on September 19, his mother Margaret lost her battle with stomach cancer. She died at the Bermondsey flat where Michael had protected her from his father all those years ago.

He had known for some months that her illness had been worsening. He had paid for treatment at London's Middlesex Hospital, grateful that he was still able to do something he had pledged as a child, to look after her in time of need. Even when he had languished in the Meadows Clinic in Arizona he had made daily transatlantic calls to check on her progress, speaking to her gently and trying to soothe her pain.

Shortly before she had been admitted to hospital, frail Margaret had given what was to be her last interview, to the *News of the World*. 'Michael's very worried about me,' she revealed. 'My illness has nothing to do with him but worry exacerbates it. I'd say Michael's more concerned about me than himself. I can't ring Michael in Arizona but he's phoned me about six times. It's causing him a lot of worry.'

It was typical of Margaret that, even in her condition, she was more concerned about her son's health than her own. 'I hope he's off the drink,' she said. 'It's vital. I hope he'll bounce back.' Then she added wearily: 'It's a shame – all those years we didn't spend together. Michael feels it. We could have had a lot of good times together.'

Michael sat at Margaret's bedside for the final hours as her life ebbed away. He held her hand and vowed: 'I'll never touch a drop of alcohol again. I'm clean and dry and I'm going to stay that way.' Margaret went to meet her maker content that the bright-eyed, eager son she had once known was back. Life had turned full circle.

The funeral was held on October 1 at The Most Holy Trinity Catholic Church near Margaret's council flat. More than 200 mourners watched as Michael, in floods of tears, was led from the service by his sister Anne. As his mum's coffin was carefully lifted into a horsedrawn carriage, Anne remained at his side supporting him as he cuddled a heartbroken nephew. Michael had sat in the front pew of the church with Anne and their brother John throughout the hour-long service.

The hymns included 'Abide With Me' and 'Here I Am Lord' and The Beatles' hit 'Hey Jude' echoed through the building as the coffin was carried out at the end. The family then followed the hearse to Honor Oak Crematorium in nearby Lewisham. Local people lined the street as the cortege set off. Flowers carried the message: 'Mum, 2 happy memories, love Baz.'

Clearly grief-stricken, Michael wept uncontrollably. His spokesman said: 'Michael is very sad indeed. You only ever get one mum.' Michael himself added later that the death of his 'hero' mother had left him feeling 'sad and lost'. He admitted that the heartbreaking blow could have been an excuse to hit the bottle again. But instead of drowning his sorrows, Michael attended two Alcoholics Anonymous meetings in one day and explained: 'I could have made myself believe I couldn't cope without a drink. Well, despite the terrible grief, I have to cope. In my mother's memory, I vow today I will never touch a drop of alcohol again.' With a wan smile he added: 'She was a very classy lady and a great deal of fun.'

The roller-coaster that is Michael's life took another sharp upturn on October 10, 2001, when he learned he would not face prosecution following the seven-month investigation into Stuart Lubbock's death. Instead he was formally cautioned under his real name of Michael Parker for possessing cannabis and for allowing it to be used in his home.

Michael received the news after he surrendered voluntarily to his police bail two weeks early. He had been due to be interviewed again on October 24.

Detective Superintendent Ian McNeill confirmed: 'Mr Parker has been released from his bail. The circumstances of Mr Lubbock's death are still under investigation and will continue until the coroner is satisfied with the file submitted by us.' It was a bald statement, as most police statements are. But for Michael, every word was a giant relief. And he subsequently released his own brief statement through David Corker. 'Michael Barrymore attended a police station at Stansted Airport this afternoon,' the statement read. 'Following a short interview, he was informed that the police investigation of him was terminated and his police bail was to be immediately cancelled. Michael Barrymore accepted a police caution in relation to the possession of a very small amount of cannabis found at his home on March 31. He was then released. Michael expressed his relief that today marks the end of any police inquiry involving him.'

The reprieve also boosted Michael's hopes of a TV comeback, though a huge question mark still hung over his career. An ITV spokesman would only say: 'We note the police's action. Michael's personal recovery continues and we have yet to make any decisions with him about his future.'

But if Michael was relieved, there was dismay etched across the face of Claire Wicks, Stuart's girlfriend and mother of his children. The 22-year-old seethed: 'I do feel that someone should be blamed. We've lost someone so lovely – but what has Barrymore lost?'

Ruth Digham, a friend of Stuart's, added: 'It's been a terrible time. All we know is that Stuart died and somebody must be held accountable.'

Three days later, the police announced that John Kenney and Justin Merritt wouldn't be prosecuted either. They were also released from bail without charge. With a sigh of relief, Justin said: 'The police told me no one could be charged with Stuart's murder. Barrymore isn't to blame. It was just a tragic accident. But,' he continued, 'perhaps he could do something for Stuart's kids to help ease the pain of losing their father.'

An overjoyed John Kenney chipped in: 'When my solicitor broke the news to me, I wanted to shout from the rooftops, "I said I was innocent!" I've been through seven months of hell over this.' He added: 'It was like somebody had taken 70 stone off my shoulders. My life's been ruined for seven months. I couldn't apply for jobs with it hanging over my head. I suffered nightmares and my health deteriorated. I'll never recover from that night. It was like something out of the movies. I kept telling myself, "You've done nothing wrong and they can't do anything to you." That kept me going, but the police don't realise what damage they've done to me and my family. My mum Margaret, who's sixty-one, is still recovering from a triple heart bypass. She hadn't been able to sleep, and when I told her police weren't taking any further action, she kept asking, "Are you sure?" Then she broke down.

'Still, though, I fear Stuart's death, and my relationship with Michael, will haunt me forever. He's my past, and one I long to forget, but I don't think I'll be able to. Nevertheless, I'm pleased Michael's not going to be charged. He's been through a rough time and I pity him. I hope for his sake he stays off the booze and drugs – especially as he made a death-bed pledge to his mother to get back on track.

'But I don't know if the public will ever be able to accept him again,' John added, voicing a thought that must have occurred to Michael himself on many occasions, 'not even on TV.'

Despite his joy at the removal of any suspicion that he had been associated with murder, though, John remained angry at the police. 'All I did was try to save a man's life,' he said. 'No one at the party that night killed Stuart. He was the victim of a tragic accident. The one thing I've learned from all this is to stay away from stars.'

When Stuart's mother Dorothy Hand learned the fate of the

three men who had been with her son that night, she became, in her own words, 'very upset and frustrated' that no one had been charged over her son's death.

'I find it unbelievable that no one has admitted what went on or has been found responsible,' she added. 'My son died and I want answers.'

Detective Superintendent McNeill stressed that the probe wasn't over yet. In another of his terse statements, he explained: 'The major investigation team is continuing to investigate the circumstances surrounding the death of Stuart Lubbock and will do so until such a time a file can be submitted to the satisfaction of Her Majesty's Coroner and/or the Crown Prosecution Service. This means we are still investigating the matter.'

On October 23 Michael made a triumphant return to the big time by winning a TV 'Oscar'. His show *My Kind of Music* was named Most Popular Entertainment Programme at the National Television Awards. But even that caused consternation among the organisers, who were reportedly concerned that there would be a blistering showdown with his ex-wife Cheryl. Both had confirmed their attendance at the Royal Albert Hall ceremony and the seating plan had Cheryl in the next row to Michael.

The pair had not seen or spoken to each other since a bust-up at the same event four years earlier. Since that 1997 clash, Cheryl had turned down every invitation to any event Michael was attending, but she would be there this year to support her client, glamour girl Lea Kristensen, whose show *The Generation Game* was nominated for Most Popular Entertainment Programme.

Michael's *My Kind of Music*, a show created by Cheryl, was nominated in the same category. A close friend of Cheryl said just before the awards: 'It's going to be a nerve-racking night for her. Anyone who knows her will tell you she's a shy and retiring person. She's not looking for a confrontation with Michael and won't be seeking him out. If he wins, Cheryl will be professionally pleased because she helped him build his TV career.'

A National TV Awards spokesman would only say: 'We're looking forward to welcoming Michael to the ceremony. It's great that he's confirmed his attendance but we've absolutely no idea what's going to happen when he gets there.'

In the event, however, Michael heeded the advice of ITV bosses and stayed away from the London ceremony. The audience fell silent as host Sir Trevor McDonald read a statement from Michael. 'In the light of recent events and the death of my mother I do not feel able to attend the awards this year,' he said. 'I really want to thank Granada and ITV for all their support. This award means a great deal to me and I want to thank everyone who voted for me.'

Michael's brother John put old enmities aside and added: 'He's very strong at the moment and trying to put everything behind him. Michael says he is desperate to make a comeback

– to do what he does best. Winning this proves the public still love him.'

However, Michael failed to win the award for Most Popular Entertainment Presenter, a category in which he had triumphed for five consecutive years. He was pipped at the post by Geordie duo Ant and Dec who hosted kids show *SM:TV*.

After the awards, Sir Trevor McDonald gave Michael his own endorsement and said he wanted to see him back on the box. 'He's too big a talent to ignore,' Sir Trevor commented. 'But I think it was right that he stayed away from the award ceremony – it was too soon.' Sir Trevor also revealed that he and Michael had talked a few hours before the show. 'We spoke for some time and he seemed fine,' he said. 'The impression I get is he's desperate to come back.'

Marcus Plantin, Granada's head of entertainment production, also gave Michael his backing. 'Michael is terrifically talented,' he said. 'With the world as it is now, more than anything else people want to be entertained, and I believe that people want him back.'

After the year from hell, Michael was poised to hit the heights once more. His next great TV performance, though, would not be on a game show. It was his explosive confessional interview with Martin Bashir.

**20**

# THE BASHIR
# INTERVIEW

THE DAYS leading up to October 30, 2001 were extremely busy ones for ITV executives. Many were told only the weekend before that there would be a late change to the schedules, a special edition of *Tonight with Trevor McDonald* screened at prime time.

Except Sir Trevor wouldn't be doing the interview himself – that would be down to Martin Bashir. Even before they knew who was being interviewed, that made the executives sit up and take notice. Martin Bashir is one of the great heavyweight interviewers of TV, famous for his groundbreaking exclusive with Princess Diana. When it became clear that this time he was going to talk to Michael Barrymore, no one complained about moving a few programmes. This was going to be edge-of-the-seat stuff.

A MAN POSSESSED

It was now seven months after Stuart Lubbock's body had been found in the Roydon mansion pool and this would be Michael's first interview about the tragedy. The chat itself was conducted in great secrecy. The two men talked for a little over three hours. Michael, in a sober, dark suit, began defensively, speaking of his early life and his rise to stardom. But under Bashir's expert probing, layer after layer of the most complex character in showbiz came away. Michael was often close to tears as he revealed secrets he had never spoken of before, sometimes not even to the psychiatrists who had treated him at the many clinics he had attended.

A handful of very senior *Tonight* executives edited down the interview to sixty minutes. But news of the programme spread and when Essex Police discovered what was going on they became worried that it might prejudice any possible trial. Officers admitted they were 'disappointed and unhappy' that Granada TV refused their request for an advance showing. Still, they decided not to seek an injunction stopping the interview.

Michael's ex-wife Cheryl warned before it was shown: 'I think it really is make-or-break time for him. How the British public react to this is crucial.'

This is Michael's full testament on the mysterious pool death as Bashir grilled him about that night. John Kenney would doubtless have been cut to the quick to hear himself described as simply 'a mate of mine who was there at the time'.

Michael strongly denied Justin Merritt's claim that he had rubbed cocaine into Stuart Lubboch's gums. He also denied that any sex took place in his mansion that night.

But he confessed he panicked and ran when he saw the dead body.

This is a full transcript of how Michael responded to Bashir's grilling over Stuart Lubboch's death.

Only where it is absolutely essential have Michael's ramblings been edited slightly to make sense of his narrative.

BASHIR: How did that evening begin? Was it a normal evening for you?

BARRYMORE: That night, the people next door and the children, we went to an Indian restaurant. We came back and I just wanted to cheer myself up. Jonathan [Kenney], who was a mate of mine, was with me at the time. I said, 'Shall we go down to a club?' And he said, 'All right.' It was just, again, on the spur of the moment. I didn't have any intention to go out to a club that night. The early part of the evening, I was going to go for the Indian meal and that was it.

BASHIR: Had you been drinking during the day?

BARRYMORE: I'd been drinking at the Indian restaurant, yeah. I'd had a few to drink by the time I got back. If you remember, I keep going on about my disease [alcoholism, the disease that, Michael insists, can control him at will], so 'a few to drink' is quite a few to most normal people.

BASHIR: So you decide to go to the Millennium club and you go with your friend John Kenney. What happened when you got to the club?

BARRYMORE: When I got to the club I walked in the door and the management looked after me straight away. They put a security guard with me, a couple to keep an eye on me. The club was busy. I was high. It was a good buzz. I had loads of girls coming up to me and I was talking to loads of blokes, it seemed like hundreds. It was getting quite heavy. Not heavy as in bad. But heavy as in it was getting a lot to deal with.

BASHIR: A bit of an event?

BARRYMORE: Yeah and I thought maybe it was a bit too much. But I ordered a drink and that and I talked to loads of people. Then, as I was leaving the club, I saw a couple of guys that I knew from the village. This bald-headed guy said, 'Oh, I'll look after you security wise and I'll take over from here.' And I went, 'Oh yeah, fine.' When we got outside he ordered a couple of taxis. I didn't know his name at the time but he was in the front of the cab. There was a girl here on my left and someone I later found out to be Stuart was sitting on the other side of the girl. And I also found out later that the girl was the bald-headed guy's sister. [It is clear, here, that Michael is referring to Justin Merritt and his sister Kylie.] And then there was another load in a car behind.

BASHIR: Had you taken any drugs that evening or during the day?

BARRYMORE: No, not during the day, or that evening.

BASHIR: So you'd only been drinking?

BARRYMORE: Yeah. I'd been drinking. I drank a Jack Daniel's and lemonade at the club and then we went back to the house.

BASHIR: The taxi driver who took you home he says, and I quote, you were 'definitely the worse for wear'. Would that be a fair description?

BARRYMORE: Worse for wear as me, or worse for wear out of everybody else?

BASHIR: No you were just the worse for wear yourself.

BARRYMORE: This is the first time I'm hearing this.

BASHIR: Just worse for wear yourself. You were quite drunk I think is what he meant as he took you home.

BARRYMORE: That's probably acceptable. I was leaning over the back of his seat talking to him. It was just another night, another club, people come back, have a drink. That's the sort of thing I did.

BASHIR: Just the sort of thing you did?

BARRYMORE: Have a drink. It was the sort of thing I did, you know... or had done.

BASHIR: And do you remember speaking to Stuart Lubbock at the club?

BARRYMORE: I don't remember particularly speaking to Stuart. I spoke to that many people, but er, I didn't know Stuart's name until after the event. [This comment would have particularly painful to Stuart's family to hear. He had died at a party thrown by a man who didn't even know his name until he was dead.]

BASHIR: But this individual who was in the cab, do you recall speaking to him in the club?

BARRYMORE: Not particularly. He was sitting on the left-hand side, on the other side of the girl. There was lots of conversation. I was talking to the cab driver most of the way. I couldn't tell you what I was talking about, but you know.

BASHIR: What happened when you got home?

BARRYMORE: We got home, I went in and showed them around the place. Not showed them round the place but, you know… there was some music in there, in the front room and that, and I said, 'Help yourself to drinks.'

BASHIR: Did you serve them drinks?

BARRYMORE: No. I didn't serve them drinks. I said, 'Help yourselves.'

BASHIR: You just showed them where the drinks were?

BARRYMORE: Yeah. I showed them where the drinks were. There's a cabinet in the front room and there's a fridge and the cooler. There was plenty of drink around and I also told them that if they wanted to use the Jacuzzi, they could.

BASHIR: Did you have to unlock the gate to allow them to get access to that?

BARRYMORE: No. It goes directly out from the kitchen and the dining room in a straight line.

BASHIR: So you just opened the door?

BARRYMORE: The door's open anyway. Just out of habit I always open the door to let in some air, or I just walk out, usually with the dogs, or I walk in the garden.

BASHIR: Admittedly you didn't know these people, but did any of the people you saw in your house appear to be drunk?

BARRYMORE: Stuart had had a drink. They'd all had drink. But nothing, nothing, nothing I would judge as so drunk that they had to be taken care of.

BASHIR: Did anybody take any drugs?

BARRYMORE: I took some drugs with a couple of them.

BASHIR: What sort of drugs?

BARRYMORE: Smoke.

BASHIR: Did you offer cocaine to anybody?

BARRYMORE: No.

BASHIR: You didn't?

BARRYMORE: No, not at all.

BASHIR: I'm sure you'll be aware that there are now effectively two descriptions of what happened on that night and both of them appear to tally.

BARRYMORE: Well, what descriptions are they?

BASHIR: Well, Justin Merritt, for example, has said that you offered cocaine to all of the people in the kitchen... and he says that you dabbed your finger in cocaine and forcibly rubbed it on Stuart Lubbock's gums in the kitchen.

BARRYMORE: That never took place. The only time I had anything was with a couple of guys down the other end of the house. And at that time they all went out to the pool.

BASHIR: Which other guys at the other end of the house?

BARRYMORE: Two of the guys. It's not for me to say who they were. I don't want to get them in trouble, unless they're answerable to the police as much as I am.

BASHIR: And what did you have with them?

BARRYMORE: Cannabis.

BASHIR: You had a smoke?

BARRYMORE: Yes.

BASHIR: So you're saying that in the kitchen you didn't give anybody or offer cocaine to anybody?

BARRYMORE: No I did not.

BASHIR: Because the description that Justin Merritt has given about you forcibly rubbing his gums with cocaine is similar to a description given by John Kenney previously where he said, 'If there is a bit of coke powder left over Michael would often dab it with his finger and rub it on his gums.' So do you remember doing that ever?

BARRYMORE: Do I remember doing that ever? I've taken

cocaine, not particularly rubbing it on my gums as such.

BASHIR: So do you think Justin… ?

BARRYMORE (interrupting): How does that tie in, I don't…

BASHIR: Well, what I'm saying is that Justin Merritt says that when they came into the kitchen you offered them cocaine and he said he didn't want any but he says he saw you dab cocaine on to your fingers and forcibly rub it into Stuart Lubbock's gums.

BARRYMORE: This… this… I've been asked this several times by the police, you know, and that's one side of the story. There's also the other side of the story, where that doesn't corroborate at all. Where Simon and James report not seeing any at all, who were with me, when we were smoking. So, you know…

BASHIR: But they weren't in the kitchen when Justin Merritt and his sister and Stuart Lubbock were with you. You said they were at the other end of the…

BARRYMORE: No. I was at the other end of the house with them. I went into the kitchen, said, 'There's the drinks, there's the music in the front room' – it's a long house, you know. But it's not that long that you can't get from one place to another. And then they decided that they were going to go in the Jacuzzi, which they did. And I showed [them] the new bit [of the house], which [the workmen] hadn't finished building on the other side. And it was at that end that we had something to smoke.

BASHIR: So is Justin Merritt lying when he says that was what you did and he saw you do it?

BARRYMORE: Is he lying?

BASHIR: Yes.

BARRYMORE: Yes he is.

BASHIR: He's lying?

BARRYMORE: Yes.

BASHIR: Even though, on a previous occasion, John Kenney recollects you doing exactly that thing – getting cocaine, dabbing it on your finger and rubbing it on your gums?

BARRYMORE: The two don't tie in.

BASHIR: Well, they tie in as something that you might do.

BARRYMORE: Something I might do?

BASHIR: Mmmm.

BARRYMORE: Not to another person.

BASHIR: It's something that John Kenney saw you do to yourself.

BARRYMORE: Yeah, you said that on another occasion.

BASHIR: Yes, and what I'm saying to you is…

BARRYMORE: That's not something that I recall ever doing.

BASHIR: You don't?

BARRYMORE: I don't know whether they're tying their stories in or not, it's not for me to speculate.

BASHIR: No, sure, but to be clear…

BARRYMORE: Yeah I'm clear about what you're saying,

I'm very clear.

BASHIR: You're saying that Justin Merritt is lying.

BARRYMORE: He is lying.

BASHIR: Given the fact that you've been honest enough to admit that you've used cocaine previously and that there are other friends of yours that recollect you buying cocaine and using cocaine, is it not possible that you had cocaine in the house that evening?

BARRYMORE: Well, it's possible that... I mean, a trace of cocaine was found in the house.

BASHIR: Is it not possible that you gave cocaine to the guests?

BARRYMORE: No. It isn't possible.

BASHIR: Why are you so categoric on that?

BARRYMORE: Because for that evening I know the sequence of events. I wasn't so off it that I didn't know what was going on. I wasn't so out of my head that I didn't know what was going on. I came into the house, showed them where everything was, went down to the other end, had a smoke with the lads, came back, went to go out to the Jacuzzi and that's when I discovered Stuart. The last time I saw Stuart was walking towards the Jacuzzi.

BASHIR: Do you remember when John Kenney got back home and the discussion you had with him when he discovered that you'd invited all these people back?

BARRYMORE: Not particularly.

BASHIR: He said that he'd had a row with you in the bedroom because he was annoyed that you'd invited people back.

BARRYMORE: Not… well… it wasn't. I don't think we had a row about it. He probably said, 'Why did you invite them back?' I probably said, 'Because I felt like it.'

BASHIR: And things were OK?

BARRYMORE: Yeah.

BASHIR: Do you remember checking on your guests and who was in the Jacuzzi? Do you remember, for example, taking out some towels to your guests? Do you remember doing that?

BARRYMORE: I probably would have done that out of courtesy.

BASHIR: Because Justin Merritt recollects that that was what you did. That you very politely and sensitively took out bath robes for everybody. Do you recollect doing that?

BARRYMORE: Yeah, I would have got the stuff out, but that would be an automatic thing, if you show someone out to the pool, to give them towels, or bath robes, or whatever.

BASHIR: So you accept that Justin Merritt is accurate when he says you took out the towels. But you reject [it] categorically when he says that you had cocaine and that you offered it to everybody and then you rubbed it on Stuart Lubbock's gums. You categorically deny that?

BARRYMORE: Yeah, and another part of that statement – that statement – was changed from his previous statement.

Why's he changing his statement? I have to question why was he changing his statement from originally, when there was no talk of any cocaine whatsoever, and then he changes his statement to when there was cocaine after being interviewed?

BASHIR: You see, the slight difficulty with the story of cocaine is that there are two people who say that now – who've given interviews, as it were, in the public domain – who say that there was cocaine that evening. That cocaine was available and that you were offering it.

BARRYMORE: Yeah and who were they? Justin, obviously.

BASHIR: And John Kenney.

BARRYMORE: Well, I haven't read those reports.

BASHIR: No. Well, both of them maintain that was what you did. And you're saying you didn't.

BARRYMORE: The two that were on charge for the murder are saying that.

BASHIR: Yes

BARRYMORE: And the two that are saying nothing about it.

BASHIR: But the two have now been released from their bail and are not being charged with murder.

BARRYMORE: Yeah. But these are reports from, well, whatever, these are reports from that time, aren't they?

BASHIR: No. The Justin Merritt interview was published yesterday.

BARRYMORE: All right.

BASHIR: All I'm saying to you is that I hope you'll understand and appreciate the wider public have heard two accounts of what happened already and now they're hearing your account. And they've heard two individuals say that you had cocaine in the kitchen and that you offered it to these individuals.

BARRYMORE: That's right.

BASHIR: Justin Merritt is saying you rubbed it in Stuart Lubbock's gums. You're saying there was no cocaine there at all. That's what you're saying?

BARRYMORE: Yes I am.

BASHIR: OK. What were you doing while the guests were outside in the pool, in the Jacuzzi?

BARRYMORE: I was down the other end of the house showing the other two guys the new bit that was built on.

BASHIR: So what happened next that raised the alarm? Can you just take me through the sequence of events?

BARRYMORE: Er... we had the smoke down there, we were there for a while, not that long... um, we agreed we'd go to the Jacuzzi and we'd give it a go. We went down to the corner end of the house. I gave them some shorts, they changed, then I changed into a pair of shorts and walked out to the pool towards the Jacuzzi, everybody was back in the house by then. And then I looked down, which was effectively the deep end, and Stuart was there.

BASHIR: Did you realise who it was?

BARRYMORE: Not, er, immediately... well I did, yeah. He was face up, yeah.

BASHIR: What did you do?

BARRYMORE: I just freaked out, I ran back in and got Jonathan, who I know was a life-saver, and Simon and James jumped in and pulled his body out.

BASHIR: Did you call the police?

BARRYMORE: No.

BASHIR: Why not?

BARRYMORE: Because somebody was doing it.

BASHIR: Justin Merritt says he dialled 999.

BARRYMORE: Yeah... Justin and Jonathan came out to the body.

BASHIR: What did you do next?

BARRYMORE: I was standing on the other side and I just lost it, I just panicked. I didn't know what to do. I couldn't believe what was going on.

BASHIR: Did you realise that the individual who was in the pool was seriously injured?

BARRYMORE: No, I had no idea. I just knew he was in the pool and that was it. I had no reason to think that at all.

BASHIR: So what did you think as you looked?

BARRYMORE: That he'd been under the water a while. From the way he was.

BASHIR: But that made you panic?

BARRYMORE: Not panic. When I say 'panic', I was just freaking out at seeing him under there, seeing that despite their efforts to do something he just wasn't coming round.

BASHIR: So what did you do?

BARRYMORE: I didn't do anything at that point. Simon and James had come down. They said, 'Get away, there's nothing that you can do', um, 'Leave the place because it's going to be swarming with police and press.' [At this point Michael allows himself a long pause.] And I just went along with that.

BASHIR: So you're saying that it was suggested to you that you should get out of the house?

BARRYMORE: Yes.

BASHIR: Do you think that was the most responsible behaviour?

BARRYMORE: No. [another pause]

BASHIR: I mean, here's a total stranger who is clearly injured in some way in the pool and you leave the house?

BARRYMORE: Yeah.

BASHIR: It's almost tantamount to a criminal offence, isn't it, your leaving the scene of an accident. Can you see that?

BARRYMORE: It's only tantamount to that if you're leaving the scene of the accident if you caused it. [There is yet another long pause, and a few stutters before Michael is coherent again.] I didn't think about what I was doing. I just didn't think what was right or wrong. They ushered me away and said to me, 'There's nothing you can do.' I said to them, 'I want to do something.' But they said to me, 'It's going to be a nightmare, just go out.' And I didn't leave straight away, without ringing my PA Mike and telling him where I was. I was not running away from the scene. If I was running away from the scene the police wouldn't have been able to find me straight away.

BASHIR: Just going back over the scene: your friends suggest that you can't be of any help. There's been this terrible incident and you don't really know what's happened, to be honest. You don't know the individual concerned, but something's happened and you're anxious about it. Some people might accuse you of running away from your responsibilities. It's your house and you've invited people to your party. Do you accept that's what it was – that you were entirely irresponsible?

BARRYMORE: I was irresponsible at the time

BASHIR: Just to leave the house?

BARRYMORE: I didn't think... [There is another pause.] I'm guilty of not thinking.

BASHIR: Again. [Here Bashir is referring to the many times that Michael has acted impulsively and got himself into trouble, usually under the influence of drink or drugs.]

BARRYMORE: Again. I didn't think, I really didn't think. I went along with somebody else suggesting what I do. What I should have done is stayed there and sorted things out. But I was in no state, I was in no state to take control. I just couldn't believe what had happened.

BASHIR: But what I'm interested in is exactly what happened to you, because that is what people want to know.

BARRYMORE: Yeah, I know.

BASHIR: That's what we're concerned about. And what happened was, you invited people to your house. It was your party and when something terrible is happening in front of your eyes, even though it was suggested to you by other people, you leave your house. That is not responsible behaviour.

BARRYMORE: No it's not at all. It is totally irresponsible and I've got to live with that.

BASHIR: You do.

BARRYMORE: I know.

BASHIR: Where did you go?

BARRYMORE: Down to Simon's flat, which is just along down the end of the... in the middle of the road.

BASHIR: OK, so you get to his flat, what's the next thing that happens?

BARRYMORE: I just sat down. Already, on the way up there, I'd phoned Mike [Brownie, his PA], told him where I was. [At this point there is another long pause as Michael takes stock of that night once again.] The guy's in the pool – I didn't know whether he was dead or not – but I was sure he was drowned. And, er, I didn't know what to do. I said, 'I'm all over the place.' My head was all over the place. I just sat there. It was just my worst nightmare, my worst nightmare become reality. I wasn't going to wake up from this one. It was the beginning of a nightmare that has been going on all this time.

BASHIR: You see, many people would say that the events of that night were bound to happen because of the way you were living. As you've said repeatedly, you were out of control, you were using drugs, you were using alcohol, you were meeting strangers and inviting them to your house.

BARRYMORE: Yeah.

BASHIR: It wasn't long before something terrible was going to happen.

BARRYMORE: Well, it was going that way, yeah. It was going headlong into something happening, if not myself ending up in that situation.

BASHIR: Do you accept that it was almost likely that it was bound to happen because of the way your life was going? It was spiralling out of control.

BARRYMORE: Well, I certainly never imagined at any time or thought that somebody would die around me – me being like I was – or in that environment. That never entered my mind.

BASHIR: When did you find out that Stuart Lubbock was dead?

BARRYMORE: Two police officers came down to Simon's flat and took a statement from me and Simon. And whilst the lady police officer was interviewing me, her walkie-talkie went and they said he was pronounced dead.

BASHIR: What was your reaction when you heard that?

BARRYMORE: I, er… [long pause] I just felt [pause] er [long pause] everything just all caved in, I just caved in emotionally and [another long pause] it was like some… some really bad film with not a happy ending.

BASHIR: What were you thinking?

BARRYMORE: I kept seeing his face [pause]. This was somebody I never knew. But it was my house, it was my pool and I felt responsible for that [long pause]. I didn't know how it happened or what happened [very long pause], you know. To this day I don't know what happened to him. I wish, you know, it could be found out so I could at least know… and his parents and family. But [long pause] it happened and – [very long pause] – whatever I say it won't [pause]… I don't know what to say, I don't know. I can't magic him up, can I? I can't… you know. Then people are coming up to me and saying, 'You didn't kill him, did you?' And I say, 'No, I didn't.' And it just dawned on me, just the enormity of everything. And that people would even think that's what I did and that's the way it was worded. If I was responsible for anything like that – and you've only got my word for it – I would put my hand up and say, 'I've done something wrong, I need help.' I would have to.

BASHIR: Stuart Lubbock was later found by the police to

have had some severe sexual injuries.

BARRYMORE: Yeah.

BASHIR: Do you know how he received those?

BARRYMORE: I have no idea whatsoever how he received them. That's another thing as well, that was the first statement – that he'd received sexual injuries. Some of the papers, or a paper, wrote, 'Sex Orgy'. But there was no sex in that house that night.

BASHIR: Not that you were aware of?

BARRYMORE: No, well in the time that I was up there… I wasn't gone that long. There was no orgy that I was aware of at all. It's totally fabricated.

BASHIR: So how did this individual come to have severe sexual injuries?

BARRYMORE: It changed from that to being an instrument. And then no instrument was found.

BASHIR: What do you mean by an instrument?

BARRYMORE: Whatever the police mean by an instrument. I don't know what the nature of these injuries were to be able to give an answer to that. I can't give an answer to something that I don't – it happened to him and I don't know what was used or if, indeed, he ever was. I'm not so sure that he actually was killed. In my mind – I've gone over and over and over it – and I can't see how it was done. And it certainly worries me that it changes from sexual assault to an instrument and to possibly now it could have been done another time. And nothing to do with that evening and it was a case of he drowned.

BASHIR: Who's told you that?

BARRYMORE: Huh?

BASHIR: Who's told you that?

BARRYMORE: Because, I've told myself that. Where else can it come from? It doesn't add up, it doesn't, there's no noise.

BASHIR: Well, speaking of noise, one of your neighbours, Lynda Clay, says that around 5 to 5.30 she was awoken by what she described as distressed screaming. She said it was hysterical, high-pitched screaming. She said, 'I thought it was an argument but there were terrible screams.' Is it possible that that was Stuart Lubbock screaming?

BARRYMORE: It's more possible that that was the screaming from the girls and from myself and from everybody just reacting to finding him. Not anything to do... the house was quiet, relatively quiet. You know, I mean it wasn't just me. There was the other two lads, the girls, why didn't they hear anything? I'm only speaking from my perspective, it doesn't add up.

BASHIR: In addition to the sexual trauma, Mr Lubbock's body was also found to have traces of Ecstasy, cocaine and Viagra. Did you provide him with any of those drugs?

BARRYMORE: No, none at all.

BASHIR: You didn't provide him with Ecstasy?

BARRYMORE: No

BASHIR: Did you provide him with those drugs at the club?

BARRYMORE: No. [long pause] It was stated, from what my understanding is, that one of his friends that was with him said he had taken those drugs.

BASHIR: Indeed

BARRYMORE: Before he went there.

BASHIR: I have to ask you the question, that's all. I accept what you're saying. It wasn't long before this terrible event had begun to unfold that you were admitted to a psychiatric hospital again. Were you running away?

BARRYMORE: Was I running away?

BASHIR: Hmmm.

BARRYMORE: No I wasn't. The police were aware of where I was going to. They were quite happy for me to go there. They didn't withhold my passport. And I was going there to get treatment, to get sorted out. To get myself well.

BASHIR: Do you see how there's a pattern where some dreadful incident occurs or there's some breakdown in a relationship or there's some kind of tragedy and then you go to psychiatric hospital and this, as it were, is the latest manifestation of that pattern?

BARRYMORE: Oh what, seeming as if they're getting me out of the way?

BASHIR: I'm only putting the question to you. Can you see why people might say, 'Oh, he's done it again, he's put himself into hospital again. An incident occurs, he admits himself into a psychiatric hospital. That's what Michael Barrymore does.'

BARRYMORE: Because, invariably, when anything happens in my life it's due to the addictions, to my disease and I have to go immediately back and get it sorted. It's not hiding away. How can I be hiding away when the police knew exactly where I am? It's for the police to decide whether I can or cannot go. I'm not above the law, I can't just do what I want.

BASHIR: How was the period while the police were investigating the incident. What was that like for you?

BARRYMORE: Well, the first rehab I went to directly after that was at Southampton. The press were outside all the time as they are... that's a part of my life I have to accept. I couldn't focus at all on any recovery.

BASHIR: So what did you do?

BARRYMORE: I just wandered around aimlessly, just going over and over in my mind and having flashbacks... of seeing Stuart. And I was distressed, totally distressed and destroyed. I wasn't even aware of myself you know. I just felt removed from myself. I just wasn't here. I just found it hard to be here.

BASHIR: Was this the lowest point of your life?

BARRYMORE: Yes, absolutely. I thought I'd hit the lows, I thought I'd hit the rock bottoms before [long pause]. I don't like having to [pause] sit here now and explain myself [pause]. I mean, I know my part. I know it. I didn't do the right thing. I should have stayed there. I shouldn't just invite people that I don't know back. That's an ongoing part of me that I need to correct and I have done over the last five months. And I want to, if not for life, to have a life. To have some sort of life. I've lost my way with my life and I... I want to find my way back.

BASHIR: What do you say to Stuart Lubbock's family and his loved ones? They've lost a partner, they've lost a father, they've lost a son. What do you say to those family members?

BARRYMORE: [long pause] I can't imagine how they're feeling. I can't begin to think where they must... where it's all going for them. I'm sorry for them. I'm terribly sorry, I'm sorry for Stuart, he didn't deserve to die. [long pause] I just hope they [pause] understand that – just another night that went terribly wrong and Stuart was there.

BASHIR: The police are saying that nobody is going to face any charges in relation to Stuart Lubbock's death. Can you see why Stuart's family feel that nobody is being held responsible for what has happened. Can you see why they feel that?

BARRYMORE: Yes I can understand that, because they were led to believe that it wasn't as straightforward as drowning. And so was I led to believe that. And if they're saying it was not a straightforward case of drowning then I, along with them, would be the first one to want to know exactly what had happened, and know it conclusively. Because what does it do, it still leaves that element. You put the word 'mystery' around it. It makes it worse because that could still imply me.

BASHIR: But isn't it true to say that if Michael Barrymore hadn't been at the centre of things that night – the Michael Barrymore who has the house, the Michael Barrymore who does invite people back, the Michael Barrymore who invites people who have had a lot to drink to use his pool, who is openly hospitable to complete strangers... Isn't it true to say that if Michael Barrymore had not been at the centre then Stuart Lubbock would still be alive?

BARRYMORE: In those circumstances, then yes, because he wouldn't have to come to the house, wouldn't have... the circumstances wouldn't have followed on. But, you know, yes, of course it's my name there all the time.

BASHIR: And it's your lifestyle.

BARRYMORE: It... it was my lifestyle. It's gonna be at the centre all the time. Yes, if I hadn't said, 'I want to cheer myself up and go out.' Yes, if Stuart hadn't been at the club that night. Yes, if people hadn't come back. It's the same as well, maybe, you know, 'Don't get in the car with me.' Am I responsible for who lives or doesn't live in an accident if I happen to be in the car?

BASHIR: Stuart Lubbock's mother at his funeral, understandably grief-stricken, said she held you partly responsible for her son's death. She said, 'It was his house, his party, his lifestyle.' Do you feel you bear any kind of responsibility for what happened?

BARRYMORE: It's my house and his mum's correct in saying that. It's my party and my lifestyle. I don't quite understand how my lifestyle, how that reflects on what happens to somebody, that is my lifestyle. I'm not saying that my lifestyle then was right, but it's my lifestyle. That has no influence or bearing on what happens directly to somebody else. Unless I was directly involved, which I wasn't.

BASHIR: Do you feel any responsibility at all for what happened?

BARRYMORE: Yes I do feel responsible. I'm responsible for the house, that's my house I'm going to. I can't not. I'm not responsible for his demise. I have absolutely no worries about that whatsoever. I have worries about how I'm perceived and how it comes across and what assumptions they're making, and how it's read and how it's written. All leading down the road of implying, always implying, implying, implying all along. I can't stop them [the press] writing that way. I can't stop them the... the...

BASHIR: His mother? The relatives of Stuart Lubbock saying what she has said – it was his house, his party, his lifestyle? She feels that you're partly responsible for her son's death.

BARRYMORE: Well, if his mum feels that, I can't stop her feeling that way can I?

BASHIR: Do you accept any responsibility?

BARRYMORE: I do accept responsibility, but only for the fact that it was my house and my pool. I'm not responsible for Stuart's death. If I was, I would say so and it would have been dealt with long before now. I've got to live, it's hard enough as it is. I'm not asking for sympathy. My disease and the way I was and my lifestyle – if you want to put it that way – got me into the situations over the years. But I'm not responsible for the way people write it, for the information that's been passed down the line and given to people which is not 100 per cent correct.

BASHIR: But you can understand, I'm sure, why people have come to that conclusion. You, yourself in this interview...

BARRYMORE: Well, why have they? Why have they?

BASHIR: Well, you yourself have admitted to a lifestyle that's barely been in control over the last thirty years. You yourself admit that you've had relationships with people that on occasions have been fleeting. You yourself admit that you've allowed people to come back to your house and you've not known who they are. You've not been in a position to be responsible for the people who are in your house because you've been out of your head yourself, as you've put it. That's why, the reason people are casting doubt on you is not necessarily, purely, because of the events of that night, but because of your history. And they say, 'This is a man who has done an awful lot of things which we know about which he himself has admitted to some extent. Therefore, it's not much of a leap to say that maybe he was responsible in some way for the death, the tragic death, of this young man.'

BARRYMORE: I totally agree with every single thing you say – that I can't find you wrong because that is the truth. What I do find wrong is the leap. I find that totally unacceptable [pause] totally, totally unacceptable.

BASHIR: Why?

BARRYMORE: Because I wasn't responsible for that. I was responsible for my behaviour and the way I was, yes. I always have been in the past. I am not responsible for this leap into thinking, 'Well, maybe he was responsible.' I've had to know where I'm coming from for me to exist.

BASHIR: It can't be very comfortable for you to know that somebody died in your swimming pool?

BARRYMORE: It's tragic. What's more uncomfortable – not more – what's equally uncomfortable is the suggestion that I had anything to do with Stuart's death.

Already Martin Bashir had got more out of Michael Barrymore than many psychiatrists had ever dreamed of getting. But there was still a little more to come. This is how the remainder of the interview went:

BASHIR: Let's talk about your future. You've been through a very intensive treatment programme in America and at this moment you're clean. Is that right?

BARRYMORE: That's right, I'm absolutely clean, yes.

BASHIR: When was the last time you drank alcohol or took drugs?

BARRYMORE: Er... a month after the, er, a month after that night.

BASHIR: So the end of April, beginning of May, was the last time?

BARRYMORE: Well, that was my relapse and then I went back into another one straight away.

BASHIR: So, since the beginning of May you haven't had any alcohol or drugs.

BARRYMORE: No, none at all.

BASHIR: In the midst of this terrible trauma, you lost your mother. That must have been very difficult for you.

BARRYMORE: It was very difficult because obviously the case had been going on all through that time, and what was sad is that she didn't live long enough to see that the charges were dropped because there was nothing to charge me with as such, with regard to what everybody was inferring. And however anybody wants to put it in the future, there never will be. Unless I become a victim, getting back to that word again, of incorrect judgements.

BASHIR: I want you to tell me how you felt when your mother died.

BARRYMORE: I just felt that I'd just lost one of the few people I had left in my life, and at the moment I haven't got that many people in my life. And I wanted her to stay around, I wanted her to live for ever and I wanted somewhere to run to. [long pause] I needed someone who believed me, like the few people I've got around me that do. Someone to know that I just muck up sometimes, I just get it wrong, but that's all that I'm guilty of, is getting things wrong.

BASHIR: What was your reaction when many commentators said that the only tears that you cried at your mother's funeral were for yourself and not for your mother.

BARRYMORE: I didn't know that comment was made.

BASHIR: A number of papers pictured you crying.

BARRYMORE: And that was the comment they made?

BASHIR: Yes.

BARRYMORE: That I was crying for myself?

BASHIR: Yes.

BARRYMORE: I feel sorry for them.

BASHIR: In a sense it's a reflection of the fact that people don't feel they can believe you any more. Do you understand that? The newspapers feel that.

BARRYMORE: How is it that my reaction from people I meet in the street, the public is vastly different from the one that is written about? How's that? Why is it that when I go out in the street over the last few months that people come up and say, 'You know we love you very much. There's a lot of love out there for you.' How is it that I get thousands of cards that say that?

BASHIR: You tell me.

BARRYMORE: No, you tell me, you're a journalist.

BASHIR: I think it's probably because many of the papers have seen you go in and out of psychiatric hospitals. They've seen you turn over another leaf and they say, 'This guy's never going to change', and they become cynical about you.

Michael hoped against hope that his interview with Martin Bashir would win over the public. But the show was beaten in the ratings by the new BBC1 drama *Linda Green*, starring Lisa Tarbuck. After 8.2 million viewers watched ITV's *Who Wants to Be a Millionaire?* only 6.5 million stayed to watch the *Tonight* interview.

And overnight viewing figures revealed that the total quickly dropped to 5.9 million before the first commercial break. In fact, it was estimated that half a million viewers turned off after watching only the first five minutes. That compared to the 7 million who watched *Linda Green*.

Viewers also rang television watchdogs to complain about Michael's excuses for his behaviour. Stuart Lubbock's mother Dorothy blasted the show for being in 'poor taste' and branded

Michael a 'coward' for running away. 'This is not about getting at the truth of what happened to my son, it's about him trying to save his career,' she added. 'My son died and I want to know how. I don't have any sympathy with Barrymore. He isn't the victim in this, Stuart is.'

Stuart's long-term partner Claire Wicks revealed she had written to Michael asking him: 'How was he on the night? Did he talk about us?' Claire, who is bringing up their children on state benefits, also revealed that she visited Michael's mansion but was rebuffed by a voice on the intercom saying: 'He may get back to you.' She told a newspaper: 'He thinks recent events have been distressing for him. Well I can't believe he's suffering a fraction of what I'm suffering.'

Meanwhile, a poll of almost 3,500 viewers for Channel 5's show *The Wright Stuff* revealed that 69 per cent of those who voted thought Michael should not return to TV. In a similar poll carried out on Teletext, more than half of those questioned thought he should not come back.

**21**

# 'SOME PEOPLE NEED COFFEE, WE NEED SEX'

AS MICHAEL went through trauma upon trauma, there must have been moments when he wished he could have the order of his old life back. Maybe not with Cheryl, because her regimes annoyed the hell out of him – and even if he had wanted her, that option was now well beyond his reach. Cheryl had carved out her own life, though she was still fated to court controversy.

A year after divorcing Michael she had been linked with camp comic Duncan Norvelle after becoming his agent. She had recruited Duncan – forty at the time – whose catchphrase was 'Chase Me, Chase Me', after seeing him perform and loving his act. But around September 1998 Duncan was spotted wining and dining Cheryl at smart London restaurants such as the Ivy. He also became a frequent visitor to her home.

Gossip went into overdrive when the pair arrived together at a showbiz party to mark the 10th anniversary of TV couple Richard and Judy. Despite his camp act, Duncan was a dad who had had romanced a string of beautiful women. These included his former girlfriend Trudie Dean, mother of his daughter Sophie, and ex-wife Tina Hall, mother of daughter Yasmin.

When news of his relationship with Cheryl hit the headlines, Duncan beamed: 'For the first time in my life I know two things for certain. I want to be a star and I've moved to London to do so. And I want to find my daughter Yasmin, who I haven't seen for many years. With Cheryl by my side, I'm going to achieve both of these things.'

If he thought the future was going to be trouble-free he was badly mistaken. Just days later Duncan was branded a 'callous rat' by fourteen-year-old Sophie.

Sophie saw the pictures of Duncan out on the town with Cheryl, read his yearning for a reunion with Yasmin, and sobbed: 'What about me?' Clutching a teddy bear that Duncan had given her when she was a toddler, Sophie hit out: 'He says he badly wants to see my half-sister Yasmin, yet he knows where I live and never comes to see me. I wish that he could take me out and make me happy like Cheryl. The last time my dad came to see me was nearly two years ago. He's missing the best years of my life and treats me like I don't exist.'

Duncan had left Sophie's mum Trudie months after their

daughter was born. He went on to marry Tina and they had Yasmin. When that relationship hit the rocks, Tina branded him a 'rotten' father and he had lost touch with his younger daughter.

'All the time my dad was married to Tina, and had Yasmin, he never contacted me at all,' Sophie continued. 'Even when he was working at a theatre in Wimbledon, just a ten-minute drive from me, he never popped in. Then, when Dad and Tina split up and he went bankrupt and lost his house, he suddenly walked back into my life again and played with my emotions.'

Duncan was in for more criticism from Trudie. She knew him inside out and was convinced that Cheryl had no idea what she was letting herself in for after the heartbreak of her split from Michael.

'I can see why Cheryl is attracted to Duncan,' Trudie told the *News of the World.* 'As soon as I met him he had me creased up laughing. But after we moved in together, I saw another side to him. I loved him so much, but while I was pregnant with Sophie I found he was having an affair with one of my best friends. I forgave him in the naive belief that he'd become a responsible father.'

After three turbulent years, the couple parted just as Duncan's TV career took off. Trudie warned Cheryl: 'The tears will outweigh the laughs, as Tina and I have found to our cost. Duncan comes across as warm and funny, but it's just a performance. He must have a heart of stone to hurt Sophie the way he has.'

Duncan would only respond to Trudie's tirade by insisting: 'There are two sides to every story.'

It was never clear if Duncan's relationship with Cheryl was more than purely business. But eventually Cheryl would find fresh, if not lasting happiness with another man, giving herself body and soul to a former male model virtually half her age. On December 7, 1998, 49-year-old Cheryl was beaming with happiness when she attended the Royal Variety Performance with 25-year-old Swiss fashion stylist Alex Rim. Looking gorgeous in a black sequinned gown, Cheryl proudly clung to her dark-haired new love – a dead ringer for a young Michael – as they arrived for the show at London's Lyceum Theatre. Prince Charles was there too.

'I'm very, very happy and in love,' she said, smiling broadly at Alex, who had also once worked as a BA air steward. 'We're very much together.'

The couple had met when Cheryl went shopping at the Versace store in London's Bond Street. Alex was working there and plucked up the courage to invite her out. Sure, she liked him, but at first she turned him down. 'I'd never been out with a younger man,' she said. 'I tried so very hard to resist him.'

But Alex was nothing if not persistent. Eventually he talked her into the date he craved and they got on like a house on fire.

So much so that within three months Alex had moved into her house overlooking Hyde Park in west London. Five days after Cheryl announced her love for Alex at the Royal Variety Performance, Michael made his quip at the British Comedy Awards about them both having toyboys – Shaun Davis for him and Alex for her.

In January 2001, Cheryl finally revealed that she and Alex were engaged. They had exchanged rings on Christmas Day. She insisted that the age difference did not matter a jot to either of them. (Cheryl is seven years older than her fiancé's mother Anita and just five years younger than his father Valentine, a textile manufacturer.)

'We had matching Cartier gold rings,' Cheryl said proudly. 'Mine was white and his was yellow. We put them in a cracker made by the jewellers Aspreys. We opened the cracker in bed, exchanged rings and Alex asked me to marry him. It was wonderful. I was unhappy for so long and now this has happened. But after all that I've been through, I think I deserve it. I'm really looking forward to being his bride. I love him and I've never been happier.'

Cheryl purred on: 'There are lots of advantages to having a younger man. Alex is perfect – and he loves sex.'

Beaming Alex also told how statuesque Cheryl turned him on. 'I love her bust,' he said appreciatively. 'Every day with Cheryl is different. There's always something new we can do sexually.' Clearly enraptured by his lady love, Alex was openly forthcoming about their more intimate moments. 'We make love in the lounge or somewhere else,' he gushed. 'I also love lingerie. I buy it for her wherever I am. We've even visited sex shops in Holland to buy it. We never get bored with each other. We simply have to make love to each other at the end of every day. Sometimes one of us is ill and we miss a day, but otherwise we always have sex. We love to play sexy games. With my other girls I have not felt this need, but I want to connect with Cheryl physically, every day. Some people need a beer or a coffee every day. For us it is sex.'

Giggling, Cheryl chipped in: 'No wonder we never go out much.'

Cheryl hadn't spoken to Michael since the National Television Awards in 1997, when he made a drunken and incoherent speech. And with the new-found emotional security of her fiancé, she recalled how the breakdown of her marriage and revelations about her husband's sexuality had once destroyed her self-confidence.

'I was completely and utterly lost,' she admitted. 'I couldn't sleep, I couldn't eat. I ended up weighing five and half stone. And I probably drank more than I should have.'

Cheryl also confessed that she and Alex had been deeply hurt by people who sneered at their romance, suggesting (albeit prophetically, as it turned out) that it would never last. 'Some people have said such unkind things about us,' she explained. 'It hurts Alex particularly. People don't know the truth about the relationship and how we feel about each other. It's upsetting – which is why I want people to know that we're getting married.'

Cheryl went on to reveal that she had bought Alex a gold Cartier love bracelet for Christmas – a band that only she could remove with a special screwdriver.

The other true love of both their lives was their West Highland terrier Gucci, which must be one of the most pampered dogs in Britain. It's named after the Italian fashion label that supplies all the pet's needs… including its bowl, bed and a jacket for cold days.

Alex and Cheryl went on record as saying that they had no plans for children. Gucci was their 'family'. Alex held his fiancée tightly and added: 'Cheryl and I will be together for the rest of our lives.'

They couldn't know at the time that their relationship had exactly a year to run. Nor could Michael. How he must have wished for what he believed was their stability. But for him, as it would for Cheryl, instability had become a way of life. And there was a new man in the offing…

# 22

# 'BEING LINKED WITH MICHAEL MEANS CROOKS KNOW WHO I AM'

HE COULDN'T help himself. Within twenty-four hours of wringing his hands in shame on TV, Michael went on a tour of London's gay haunts. There was no way he was going to keep it a secret, he was one of the most recognisable figures on the circuit. And when news broke it caused outrage.

He hit the town with a handsome 21-year-old called Dan Lichters. They arrived at the Ku Bar in the West End shortly before 9 p.m. Throughout the evening Michael was seen running his hand up and down Dan's leg. And, as usual, there were the hangers-on. Michael couldn't resist playing to the gallery and even had the nerve to joke about his TV broadcast – complaining that it had made him look podgy.

As he prodded his chin, crowds who knew nothing of the

Lubbock family's pain, roared with laughter when Michael announced: 'See, I'm not really that fat! The cameras were lying.'

Asked about his decision to go partying so soon after sharing his sorrow on screen, Michael brazened it out. 'You can't go on sulking on your own forever,' he maintained. 'I came out tonight to have a laugh. I needed to.' No one in Stuart Lubbock's family was laughing, but Michael was on a roll. 'It's good to be here,' he went on. 'It helps. I'll never be able to forget what happened, but I can't let it do me in.'

Shortly after 11 p.m. Michael and his party left the Ku Bar and headed to the nearby Heaven nightclub, where they stayed till 3 a.m.

Dan and Michael had been pictured out shopping in London's Knightsbridge a few days earlier. At the time no one knew who Dan was, but it didn't take long for seasoned Barrymore watchers to build up a full picture of the new bloke at his side. And in a gift to the newspapers, he turned out to be a policeman. Not just any policeman but a Gay and Lesbian liaison officer with the Met!

Dan, or PC Lichters as they knew him in Kentish Town nick, carried out his liaison duties out of hours. His other claim to fame, besides being spotted with Michael, was that he had once been the youngest policeman in Britain. Dan, who is originally from Gloucester, went on the offensive. 'I'm gay,' he said. 'Any officer in London will tell you that I'm totally "out" and make no secret of it. I am also, of course, fully aware of Michael's situation. But my relationship with him has absolutely no bearing on the police inquiries he has been involved in. I don't want to say whether we're just good friends or anything like that. I prefer to say nothing.'

Dan's colleagues said the relationship was 'the talk of the station' and it emerged that he had been taken off plain-clothes duties with the Robbery Squad because now that he had appeared in the papers his cover had been blown. 'Being publicly linked with Michael means the crooks around Camden and King's Cross know who I am,' he explained. 'People recognise me all the time.' Michael had had that problem for ages. But while he might have been having a good time at the Ku Bar and Heaven, he wildly overestimated the patience of his ITV bosses. They were furious at his late-night revelry. The official word was that Michael's career was 'on hold' while he got over the pool scandal and the death of his mother. But an ITV source confided: 'To say that Michael didn't do himself any favours prancing about town so soon after the Bashir interview would be a bit of an understatement! He's irritated a number of senior ITV executives by his actions. He told everyone he was a reformed character and was fit, ready and eager to get back to work, but after the Bashir interview he went straight back to his old gay haunts and even had a gay policeman on his arm. You couldn't make it up!'

Michael was given a severe warning about his behaviour from one female Granada executive. The ITV source added: 'Let's say she had a "few words" with Michael about his behaviour, though she didn't get a very positive response back from him! All we want is for him to use a bit of common sense, but Michael simply can't see what he has done wrong and just thinks the world is against him. It's unbelievable, but that's the person we're dealing with. Unless someone is holding his hand the man is still a loose cannon.'

But loose cannon or not, he still had his value as an entertainer. ITV bosses, struggling in the ratings war with the BBC and painfully aware that *My Kind of Music* had won the Most Popular Entertainment Programme at the National TV Awards, finally decided that he was too big a star to let go.

That same month, November 2001, Michael secretly signed a £300,000 deal to host a new series of *My Kind of Music*. LWT said filming would begin in the New Year with transmission in 'Spring at the earliest.' Michael was jubilant – and not just because his career had been saved... By now Dan Lichters was history and Michael had got back with his 'husband' Shaun Davis. Dan only found out about it when he read the newspaper reports.

Nine months after they had parted so acrimoniously, Shaun had flown back from his home in New Zealand for a make-or-break reunion. Michael spent £4,000 on a romantic weekend in the Gleneagles hotel in Perthshire to woo back his ex-lover. They spent three romantic days together in a £700-a-night suite. Both of them, of course, knew the hotel well. They had stayed there before, when Michael had chased Phil Stanyon around the hotel so ardently that the worried man had had to change the number on his door.

But old problems were quickly forgotten, and when 26-year-old Shaun agreed to give their 'marriage' a second go Michael bought him a £12,000 Mini Cooper. On their return south, Shaun promptly moved back into the Roydon mansion. It is unclear whether all the old pictures of Shaun, removed when John Kenney found them unsettling, had been polished up and returned to their original places.

A friend said: 'Michael apologised to Shaun for his previous behaviour and blamed it all on booze and drugs, but he insisted he was now completely off the drink and drugs and was a reformed character. Shaun believed him and was totally bowled over. But it can't have been easy for Shaun to move back into the Roydon house. After all, he moved out just days before Stuart Lubbock drowned.'

Michael was in ebullient mood, however, and the Mini for Shaun wasn't the only treat on the menu. He had also bought himself a £3,000 bubble car because it reminded him of the first car he'd ever bought – a blue two-seater bubble car. 'I remember that bubble car so well,' Michael's mum had once recalled. 'He used to take me shopping in it. He'd be driving and I'd be in the back with all the shopping bags.'

Now, decades later, car-mad Michael snapped up the classic 1958 three-wheeler Heinkel Cabin Cruiser after seeing it advertised in a newspaper. He squeezed his 6-foot-3-inch frame into the motor to pose with a chum and was like a kid with a new toy. It was just 6 foot long and had a top speed of 40mph – rather different to his Bentley.

The previous owner was 22-year-old journalist Jonathan Smith from Highgate, North London, who told how Michael had fallen in love with the car at first sight: 'He rang about the ad,' said Jonathan. 'I was amazed when he said who he was. He got really excited as soon as he saw the motor – he started running around it when I handed over the keys. He was desperate for a test drive and said he'd always loved bubble cars because they're so strange-looking. You climb in through the front and he looked funny getting in because he's so tall. I guess he was taking his mind off his recent troubles by cheering himself up.'

Michael and Shaun ended 2001 on another high note, taking a friend's three grandchildren on a three-day Christmas break to Disneyland Paris. The kids, a thirteen-year-old boy and twin girl and another boy aged eight, whooped with delight as they went on white-knuckle rides and met Disney favourites Mickey Mouse and Goofy.

Michael's PA Mike 'Brownie' Brown and his wife and son also made the trip to France. A spokeswoman for Michael said: 'He absolutely loves children. He's having these three to his house for Christmas and has used the trip to stock up on presents for them.'

But these were all distractions from what would always be the main part of Michael's life – performing on stage and TV. Explaining why he had delayed his TV comeback, Michael told the press: 'It's out of respect for Stuart and his family. There's a right time. It would be wrong for me to have come back from treatment in America, for example, and bang – suddenly I'm on the next week smiling and jumping around. I know there are millions of people that want me to go back up there. It's just a timing thing.'

And would the old magic still be there?

'I'll be honest with you, I'm frightened,' he admitted. 'I'm terrified. 'The bravado's all gone, you know.'

January 2002 was a time of uncertainty and upheaval for ex-wife Cheryl too, as she left it to close friends to announce that her relationship with Alex Rim was over. One pal admitted: 'It is true. They have split. But there's genuinely no one else involved. It just wasn't going anywhere and it ran out of steam. Yes, at one stage they were planning to get married, but things change. It's been a gradual thing over the past few months as they saw less and less of each other. A lot of it is because Cheryl has been so busy developing a new series and Alex is travelling a lot. They just drifted apart.

'With the start of the New Year she and Alex finally made up their minds to call it a day. They remain friends and they'll still see each other but they're no longer an item. Just mates.'

The friend added: 'It's taken Cheryl an awful long time to get over Michael and I think the situation with Alex achieved that. Now she's back on her feet and having a lot of success with a new series coming up, she realised that the relationship wasn't what she thought it was.'

But was there any chance of a reconciliation with Michael?

'Absolutely not,' said the friend. 'There's no way Cheryl would ever get back with Michael. He doesn't even come into the conversations any more. I know you can never say never about anything but she has nailed that particular situation and got her confidence back. I think Cheryl is more positive and buoyant than she has been for years.'

A friend of Michael's confirmed that he felt the same. 'He told me he hasn't felt so happy in years,' said the pal. 'He and Shaun are getting on brilliantly. There's no way he'd get back with Cheryl, she controlled his life too much. Anyway, I think Shaun is great for him – 2001 was a terrible year for Michael, but he insists he's finally beaten his demons and has given up the booze and drugs for good.

'He's looking forward to the future.'

And what was that about losing his bravado? Well, maybe it's only temporarily. In the same month, a relieved Michael finally made his long-awaited TV comeback. As he filmed his new series of *My Kind of Music* at LWT's studios on London's South Bank, the 500-strong audience gave him a rapturous reception.

Two words shouted to his fans brought the curtain down on his nightmare year: 'I'm back!'